Change and Tradition
Cultural and Historical Perspectives

The
Ancient Greeks

Emma Lou Thornbrough

Butler University

Copley Publishing Group
Acton, Massachusetts 01720

CONTENTS

MAPS

CHRONOLOGICAL TABLE

All Dates Are B.C.

c. 1600	Height of Minoan Civilization
c. 1400	Height of Mycenaean Civilization
c. 1184	Fall of Troy
c. 1100–750	Greek Middle Ages
c. 800	Homer
776	First Olympic Games (traditional date)
c. 750–550	Colonization
c. 750–500	Archaic Greek Civilization
594	Solon archon at Athens
560–527	Tyranny of Peisistratus
545	Persian conquest of Asiatic Greeks
508–507	Reforms of Cleisthenes
499–494	Ionian revolt against Persia
490	Battle of Marathon
490–456	Plays of Aeschylus
480s	Athens builds fleet
c. 480–430	Herodotus
480	Battles of Thermopylae and Salamis
479	Battle of Plataea
477	Delian League established
468–406	Plays of Sophocles
c. 460–400	Thucydides
455–406	Plays of Euripides
454	Treasury of Delian League moved to Athens
448	Athenian Empire established

447	Parthenon begun
c. 460–429	Pericles *strategos*—leader of Demos
431	Outbreak of Peloponnesian War
427–347	Plato
c. 424–388	Plays of Aristophanes
421	Peace of Nicias
415–413	Athenian expedition against Syracuse
411–410	Oligarchic revolution of the 400 at Athens
404	Athens surrenders to Sparta
404	Thirty Tyrants at Athens
403	Restoration of democracy at Athens
399	Trial and death of Socrates
384–322	Aristotle
377	Second Athenian Confederacy
359–336	Reign of Philip of Macedon
338	Battle of Chaeronea
336–323	Reign of Alexander the Great
323–276	Wars of Alexander's generals; break-up of his empire
336–31	Hellenistic era

PART I

INTRODUCTION

We begin our study with the ancient Greeks for two reasons. In the first place, these Greeks were one of the most original and creative people of all time. Their literature, institutions, religious beliefs, art, and philosophy are intrinsically worth studying in themselves. In the second place, much of what we call "western civilization" is the legacy of ancient Greece, transmitted in part by the Romans. A study of the contributions of the Greeks to later cultures would include much of the history of the western world. In the United States in the twentieth century there are many evidences of the Greek heritage although perhaps many Americans do not recognize them.

For example, one of the things which modern Americans share with the ancient Greeks is their enthusiasm for athletics and sports. The first Olympic Games were held in Greece at least as early as 776 B.C., and many of the contests and events at the Olympics today have their origins in the Greek games.

The Greeks invented drama and the theater, and although modern dramatic productions are in many respects very different from the ancient festivals, the development of theater throughout history has been influenced by Greek standards and practices. Many modern playwrights have drawn upon the themes and plots of the ancient Greek dramatists. Examples from the twentieth century are Jean Anouilh's *Antigone* and Eugene O'Neill's *Mourning Becomes Electra*.

Greek literature—the epic poems of Homer, the lyrics of Sappho, the tragedies of Aeschylus, Sophocles, and Euripides, the histories of Herodotus and Thucydides, the dialogues of Plato—is universally regarded as one of the greatest of all time. The writings of the Greeks have furnished inspiration and models for western literature throughout the centuries, and the stan-

3

dards set forth by Aristotle continue to influence literary criticism.

Even more obvious has been the Greek influence on architecture. The so-called "classical" tradition has been important from the Renaissance to the present. The sculptures of the fifth and fourth centuries B.C., many of which adorned the temples, the greatest achievement of Greek architecture, are still regarded as the finest ever wrought. Our values and ideals for all the visual arts are derived largely from Greece.

More important perhaps than these concrete examples of the Greek legacy are intangibles, the ways of thinking and ethical and moral values of the Greeks. The influence of Greek thought as reflected in literature generally and in philosophy in particular has been of incalculable importance. Among ancient societies Greece was the first to give freedom for individualism and individual expression. But the individual Greek was always a part of society, and Greek thought was concerned with the place of the individual in society and in relation to the state, as well as with questions of individual ethics.

While their achievements in science and in scientific research were limited, the ancient Greeks may be said to have developed scientific ways of thinking and the scientific method. If the answers to the riddles of the natural world and the nature of humankind provided by the philosophers and scientists were not always accurate, Greek thinkers asked the right questions. Rejecting the traditional answers of myth and mystery, they invented the scientific method of close observation, measurement, and experiment. And when Plato says that "God is always doing geometry," he reveals a concept of Greek origin without which modern science, philosophy, even musical notation would be impossible. The great contribution of the Greeks was the belief that the universe was rational and that human beings could discover its nature by asking rational questions.

We begin our study of the ancient Greeks by asking some questions of our own. Who were the Greeks? Where did they live, and how did their land, its geography and climate, affect the development of Greek culture? The focal point of our attention will be Greece, and Athens in particular, in the fifth and fourth centuries B.C. This is usually known as the "classical" period, the period of the greatest intellectual and artistic achievements.

While studying about the Greeks and other past civilizations we must remember that we can never have the complete story. What we know depends upon the evidence that survives. The most important evidence is usually written records, but these are often fragmentary and incomplete and sometimes of doubtful authenticity. They must be supplemented by other evidence. The traditions of a people are also important in understanding their past, and the study of physical remains as revealed by archaeology supplements and corroborates or modifies written records and oral traditions.

GEOGRAPHY

The Mediterranean World

For many centuries the Mediterranean Sea was the center of western civilization. The homeland of the ancient Greeks was on the southern portion of the Balkan peninsula and the surrounding islands in the Aegean and Ionian seas. But the Greeks roamed the entire Mediterranean. From very early times there were Greek settlements on the coast of Asia Minor. Later colonies were founded in southern Italy, Sicily, and as far west as southern France. In the east Greeks settled around the shores of the Black Sea. Greek civilization developed around the fringes of the Mediterranean, never penetrating far into the interior. The location of the Greek mainland in the eastern Mediterranean where there were contacts with the older civilizations of the Middle East was no doubt one reason for the early development of Greek civilization.

The Mediterranean is a vast sea, almost entirely cut off from other bodies of water. The narrow straits of Gibraltar between the southern tip of Spain and the north coast of Africa were a natural outlet to the Atlantic Ocean. Until the building of the Suez Canal in the nineteenth century, linking the Mediterranean to the Red Sea and the Indian Ocean, there was no access by water from the Mediterranean world to the lands of the Far East. Narrow straits connect the Mediterranean with the Black Sea, an inland sea.

The Mediterranean Sea itself is divided into smaller basins by straits between mainland peninsulas and islands. Three large mountainous peninsulas jut into the Mediterranean from the north: the Balkan, farthest east, the Italian in the center, and the Iberian in the west. The sea is dotted with islands, most of them of the same rocky, mountainous character as the mainland. The largest island, Sicily, south of Italy, is separated from the mainland by narrow straits. The second largest, Crete, lies south of the Greek mainland. Farther east, close to the Asian shore, is Cyprus. Smaller islands abound, especially in the eastern Mediterranean.

The lands surrounding the Mediterranean and the islands form a distinct geographical area, shut off from the hinterlands by natural frontiers: by mountain ranges along the northern borders of the Balkan, Italian, and Iberian peninsulas and by the desert and mountains of the African interior.

The climate of the Mediterranean world is sub-tropical, with hot, dry summers and rainy, relatively mild winters.

Because of the mountainous terrain and lack of navigable rivers, the Greeks became a maritime people, trading and communicating by sea in fragile wooden vessels. The Greeks sailed principally along the coastline and from island to island, navigating to land sightings in the brilliantly clear summer atmosphere.

Greece: The Land

Greece is a country of spectacular beauty. From Homer forward, poets have celebrated its majestic mountains and its glorious sea, here "wine-dark," there a brilliant turquoise. The natural beauty of Greece and her artistic heritage attract thousands of tourists every year.

The land of Greece, mainland and island, is the product of a relatively recent geological era, as frequent earthquakes and tremors attest. To the ancient Greeks, Poseidon, god of the sea, was also Poseidon, "earth shaker."

Other clearly defined regions of ancient Greece include Macedonia, Epirus, and Thrace to the north, all inhabited by peoples of the same ethnic and linguistic stock as the Greeks themselves. The Greeks of classical times, however, did not regard these peoples as part of Hellas.

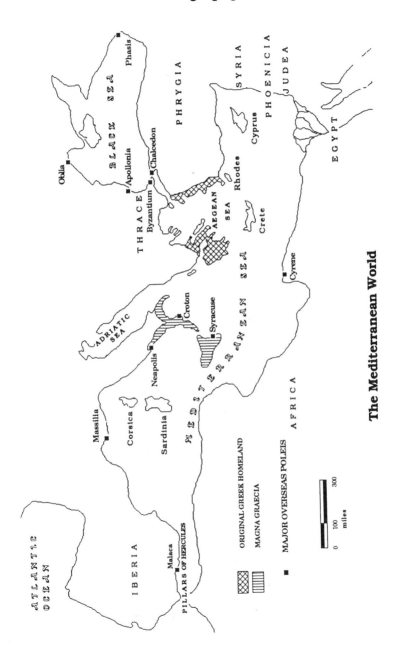

The Mediterranean World

Greek Homeland

Important regions that were regarded as part of Hellas include Thessaly in the north, surrounded by mountains, with
broad plains and colder temperatures not typical of the rest of
Greece. Just off the coast was the large island of Euboea, once a
part of the mainland. Central Greece included Boeotia and the
famous city of Thebes, and Phocis, where Delphi and the oracle

of Apollo were located. South of Boeotia, the city-state of Athens embraced the entire area of Attica.

The narrow isthmus of Corinth separated the Peloponnesus, the southern part of the mainland, from central Greece. Corinth, on the Bay of Corinth, was one of the more important city-states. Farther south in the Peloponnesus was the site of ancient Mycenae, the center of the earliest mainland civilization. The southeastern segment of the Peloponnesus was Laconia, the Spartan state. In the northwest was Olympia, where the games were held.

Myriad small islands, including the chain known as the Cyclades, encircling the sacred island of Delos, dot the Aegean Sea to the east of the Greek mainland. Farther east, off the coast of Asia, were island city-states—Lesbos, Samos, Chios, and Rhodes. On the coast of Asia were other Greek city-states, among them Miletus, a center of trade and industry and the mother city of colonies.

Geography and climate are important in shaping the history and institutions of any country, but their importance for the development of ancient Greece is especially apparent. Except for a few high, snow-capped peaks such as Mount Olympus in the north and Mount Ida in Crete, the mountain ranges were not high, but they divided the mainland and the islands into many valleys, geographically isolated. Valley plains were shallow and rocky, better for the growing of barley than wheat. Lack of arable land led to the importation of grain in early times, and eventually to overseas colonization.

Two crops for which Greece is well-suited, olives and grapes, provided staples for the Greek diet as well as excellent export commodities. No sight is more typical of the Greek landscape than groves of olive trees, many of the trees centuries old and gnarled with years. Oil from the olive was used for cooking and as fuel for lamps. Vineyards, planted along terraced slopes, produced the universal drink—wine diluted with water.

Sheep and goats grazed the hillsides and mountain slopes. Sheep were raised for their wool; both sheep and goats for their milk. Flocks grazed on the lower slopes over the mild winters, then were taken to the highlands in summer. Only at special times, on occasions of celebration or sacrifice, was the meat of the animals eaten.

The economy of ancient Greece was based primarily on agriculture, but farming was supplemented by other occupations. Abundant resources of clay encouraged pottery-making. Ceramic art flourished early and Greek ware was found all over the Mediterranean. Fine stone was quarried for building and architecture, the finest white marble from Mount Pentelicus in Attica.

Generally poor in metal and mineral resources, Greece imported tin for the making of bronze. Gold and iron were scarce, but fifth century Attica saw the opening of rich lodes of silver. Today the hills of Greece are largely denuded of timber but there were some forests in ancient times, harvested for fuel and for building, including ship building.

If the farmland of Greece was poor, the sea was an abundant provider—of fish and salt, and of purple mollusks highly prized for dye-making. Although the Greek mainland is only one-third the size of Italy and one-sixth that of the Iberian peninsula, the coastline of Greece is longer than either. From earliest times the sea was an avenue for travel and trade and for emigration to new lands. The later greatness of Athens rested on her pre-eminence as a naval power. Indeed, until the rise of Rome, sea power was decisive in the warfare of the Mediterranean world.

Geography and climate were important, also, in shaping government and style of living for the Greeks. Small groups, isolated from their neighbors in the mountainous land, developed local pride and intense loyalty to a small political entity, the *polis*. Typically Greek, the *polis* was regarded by the Greeks as the ideal state. The mild climate fostered an outdoors life. Government assemblies, dramatic festivals, athletic contests—all were out-of-doors events. Greek men spent little time at home, and domestic architecture was not important. Resources were lavished, instead, on public places, temples especially, in honor of the *polis* and its gods.

The People

The people whom we call the ancient Greeks called themselves Hellenes. The name *Greek* comes to us from the ancient Romans who first encountered Hellenes in settlements in southern Italy, a region the Romans called Magna Graecia (Great Greece). There was no geographical entity called Greece or Hellas. The term *Hellas* was applied to the Hellenes as a people collectively.

The Hellenes had neither a nation (like modern Greece) nor the modern sense of nationalism, but they were very conscious of their identity as a distinct people, "being of the same stock and the same speech, [with] common shrines of the gods and rituals, [and] similar customs," as the historian Herodotus said (VIII, 144). So strong was their sense of a common identity that the Greeks used the term "barbarians" to designate all non-Hellenic cultures. Nevertheless, as important as was this abstract concept of Hellas in shaping Greek civilization, it did not prevent Hellenes from fighting and enslaving one another.

According to Greek tradition all Hellenes were descended from a common ancestor called Hellen. In reality, Greeks from the earliest times were a mixed people. About 1950 B.C., invaders from the north who spoke an early form of the Greek language entered the territory of modern Greece. Thereafter, over a period of centuries (Probably until about 1000 B.C.), Greek-speaking peoples continued to make their way southward into the Greek mainland and the islands. Evidence of pre-Greek inhabitants is found in some words in the Greek language and in place names. Inconsistencies in Greek mythology and religion of the classical period are probably the result of the mixture of early peoples and cultures.

The Greek language of classical times belongs to the Indo-European group of languages, a far-flung family which includes Latin, Germanic, ancient Persian, and Sanskrit. The Greek alphabet was adopted from the Phoenicians, who inhabited what is modern Lebanon on the east coast of the Mediterranean. The Phoenicians, a sea-faring, commercial people, used their writing for business purposes. Perhaps as early as 700 B.C., the Greeks

had adapted the Phoenician alphabet to their language success-
fully enough to produce the first written versions of the Homeric
epics.

A SURVEY OF GREEK HISTORY
TO 500 B.C.

Oral tradition and legend were important in shaping the Greeks' ideas about their past and their perceptions of themselves, but they had no system of writing before 700 B.C., and such written evidence as exists for the next 200 years is fragmentary. Today, as the result of archaeological discoveries, we know far more about the early history of the ancient Greeks than they knew about themselves. The discoveries of Heinrich Schliemann in the late nineteenth century at the legendary site of Troy on the coast of Asia Minor (modern Turkey) and the Greek mainland at Mycenae opened a new era in historical scholarship. Schliemann's discoveries and those of his successors appeared to substantiate the authenticity of places and possibly events described in Homer's *Iliad*. A few years later, Sir Arthur Evans, like Schliemann an amateur who invested his own personal fortune in his excavations, discovered a magnificent palace and remains of a still earlier civilization at Knossos on the island of Crete. The civilization he discovered came to be known as Minoan from the name of the legendary king of Crete, Minos. The term Mycenean designates the civilization of Schliemann's discoveries.

Subsequently, professionally trained archaeologists continued excavations at the sites discovered by Schliemann and Evans, excavating other sites on the Greek mainland, Crete, and other islands. Their discoveries have vastly expanded our knowledge of the so-called "pre-history" of Greece.

Our knowledge of the period following the decline of Minoan and Mycenaean civilizations to the beginning of the fifth century B.C. rests largely on legend and archaeological evidence. For the fifth and fourth centuries much more abundant written evidence exists, but archaeology continues to supplement, rein-

15

force, and sometimes modify our knowledge and understanding of classical Greece.

The Bronze Age—Minoan and Mycenaean Civilizations

Some time after 3000 B.C. a Bronze Age culture developed on Crete. Bronze, an alloy of copper and tin, was used for tools, weapons, and utensils, made earlier of copper and still earlier of stone. Although some basic skills in metalwork may have been brought from earlier civilizations in the east, Minoan civilization is regarded as being largely a native development. It reached its most brilliant period from about 1950 to about 1550 B.C. Archaeology has revealed a magnificent palace at Knossos and smaller palaces at other points on the island. The palaces, not only royal residences but also centers of administration and industry, contained workshops for artisans and huge storerooms for such commodities and articles of trade as oil and grain.

Archaeological evidence suggests a long period of peace and a sea-faring kingdom. There were no fortifications and there are many evidences of trade over a large part of the Mediterranean. The palace was apparently the center of a highly centralized bureaucratic system through which the ruler dominated the economy, collected taxes in kind from an agricultural population, and probably had a monopoly on trade. Skilled artisans produced bronze weapons, ceramic pottery, and probably textiles for export. A mature, sophisticated, naturalistic art developed, including beautifully decorated eggshell pottery and exquisitely decorated weapons and gold jewelry. Frescoes which decorated palace walls portray fish, flowers, and birds, and provide glimpses of the luxurious life and recreations of the upper classes. The women pictured are dressed in costumes quite different from those of classical Greece. In the classical period women wore loose fitting robes fastened at the shoulder; in Minoan frescoes women are pictured in bosom-revealing dresses with tight waists and full skirts.

Religious objects, including figurines of a famous snake goddess and votive offerings found in caves, suggest some of the religious beliefs and practices. Later Greek religion retained elements inherited from the Minoan past.

Somewhat later, the mainland civilization known as Mycenaean developed. The Mycenaean Greeks, probably an amalgam of petty kingdoms, were the Achaeans of the poems of Homer, bitter foes to the Trojans. Both literary and archaeological evidence suggests a warlike people, ruled by wealthy kings and nobles, their settlements grouped around fortified citadels.

Though relations between Minoans and Mycenaeans continue to puzzle scholars, some cross-cultural influence seems certain. While arts and metalwork found on the mainland show Minoan influence, linguistic evidence suggests that invaders from the mainland dominated Crete for a period after c. 1500 B.C. Important evidence is the system of writing known as Linear B. Tablets in this writing have been discovered on both Crete and the mainland. It has been deciphered as an early form of Greek, the language spoken by the Mycenaeans.

The reasons for the decline and virtual disappearance of these two early civilizations are matters of uncertainty and controversy. Various theories have been advanced, including natural disasters such as earthquakes (in the case of Knossos), possible invasions by both land and sea, social revolution, and wars between the petty kingdoms. Whatever the causes, there is evidence of devastating physical destruction of palaces and fortifications, virtual disappearance of some centers, and a general decline in population and the level of culture. Writing disappeared completely so far as we know. This period is sometimes called the Greek "dark ages."

During this era of upheaval there was also a dispersal of Greeks—possibly in the face of foreign invaders. Many Greeks from the mainland settled on the coast of Asia. These settlers and their descendants kept alive, through oral tradition, memories of the "golden age" of Mycenae and its heroes. Homer draws his epic from these memories.

Homer

The *Iliad* and the *Odyssey*, the two earliest surviving examples of European literature, were composed in that shadowy, transitional period when the Greeks were emerging from the "dark ages" into a new era—some time in the eighth century B.C. The subject matter of both poems is drawn from the legends about the war between the Greeks and Trojans which, according to tradition, began about 1200 B.C. and lasted for ten years. The *Iliad* is not a narrative of the entire war. It centers on a ten-day period—on a quarrel between two Greeks, the mighty warrior Achilles and Agamemnon, King of Mycenae, and the consequences of their quarrel for the Greeks and the Trojans. The *Odyssey* tells of the wanderings and adventures of another Greek hero, Odysseus, who finally returns to his home and his faithful wife, Penelope, and of their son Telemachus, who leaves home in search of his missing father.

Whether the man Homer actually existed, whether the same person composed both poems—a complex of issues known as the "Homeric question"—has been the source of much scholarly debate. We do know, however, that the tales of the *Iliad* and the *Odyssey* were not original with Homer. Instead, they developed through generations of oral tradition and oral poetry about a heroic past, told and retold by skilled singers or *bards*. The Homeric poems preserve the culmination of this oral process, providing a fascinating link between the old and the new.

These epic poems had an incalculable influence on later Greek thought and culture. Next to their common language, the poems were the most important common heritage of all Greeks. They were central to the education of the Greek boys and countless Greeks could recite parts of them from memory. Homer was considered by later generations as the authority for religion and history. The poems reflected the values of the heroic society about which Homer wrote and influenced later ideas about ethics and morals. The hero Achilles embodied physical courage and prowess, loyalty to friends, and the ideal of personal honor which required that insults be avenged. The wily Odysseus possessed other qualities which the Greeks admired—resourcefulness and quick-wittedness—as well as valor. Each in his own way, these heroes represent a particular Greek concept of virtue—*arete* or excellence. For the Homeric hero, the life-long striving for *arete* means, in particular, the fulfilling of duties toward oneself.

The Archaic Age

The archaic age (c. 800 to c. 500 B.C.) is important as a formative period which prepared the way for the developments in the fifth and fourth centuries. During this period the alphabet came into use and writing revived, though few written documents have survived. Historians must rely on fragments of poetry, tradition as reflected in the writings of a later age, and archaeology.

Social Organization

At the heart of Greek society was the family or household (*oikos*). The primary institution through which most of life was organized, the family assured continuity by providing male heirs who would inherit and conserve property for future generations. Blood relationship and legitimacy were of great importance. Citizenship, the right to inherit land, and participation in the state and religious rites depended upon belonging to a family.

Related families were grouped into a larger unit, a brotherhood (*phratra*), and these in turn were grouped into a larger unit, the tribe (*phyle*), which was the basis of military organization and participation in government. In a relatively primitive society, in which administration of justice was largely a private rather than a public matter, membership in a brotherhood was important. A person without family ties was an outcast. Although Greeks placed great emphasis upon the obligations of hospitality, outsiders were suspect and excluded from the community which formed the Greek state.

In this society women derived their status from their fathers or husbands. By law and custom women were subordinate to men, but there is reason to think that women in the archaic period enjoyed greater freedom than in classical Athens.

Slaves were a part of the population of every Greek state. Although the form of servile labor varied, slavery was taken for granted in archaic Greece as in every period of Greek history. Most of the slaves at this time were probably persons captured in war and their descendants. In an agricultural society most slaves worked on farms, usually small holdings worked by a farmer and one to two slaves.

Government—The Polis

After the decline of the small kingdoms of the Mycenaean period, Hellas fragmented further into hundreds of tiny sovereign states. The *polis,* the name given to these states, was the distinctive and characteristic feature of governmental organization in archaic and classical Greece. The usual translation of *polis* as "city-state" is misleading. The *polis* consisted of an urban community, sometimes only a walled village, and the surrounding countryside. The *polis* did not develop in some of the more remote parts of Greece, in the primitive regions in the north in particular, but the Greeks viewed the *polis* as the only civilized system of government and as an institution which distinguished them from barbaric peoples.

The *polis* was formed by the concentration of population at some easily defensible site, usually around an acropolis (which literally means "high city"). Often it was located on an earlier Mycenaean site. Throughout its history ancient Greece remained primarily a rural, agrarian area, and most of the population of the *polis* were farmers who lived in town or village and went to the countryside daily. The amount of territory embraced in a *polis* varied greatly. Athens and Sparta, two large states about which we know most, were not typical. Some of the states were remarkably tiny. For example, some of the small islands included a number of states. Hundreds of these states developed on the Greek mainland and islands and the coast of Asia Minor and, as Greeks planted colonies in more distant lands, their number grew.

Each *polis* was an entirely independent sovereign state. Each had its own government, its own laws, its own local gods and religious cults, its own system of money. According to Aristotle the ideal *polis* was large enough to be self-sufficient; small enough to be neighborly:

> But there is also a proper measure for the size of a city, just as there is for everything else—animals, plants, instruments. For all these will exercise their proper function only if neither too small nor excessive in size. . . . Similarly with a city: if it is made up of too few it will not be self-sufficient (and cities are self-sufficient); if it is made up of too many, it will be self sufficient in necessities (the way whole peoples are), but it will not be a city. . . . And who will be military commander of a crowd so excessive? Who will be herald unless he have the voice of Stentor? . . . As for making judgments about what is just and assigning public office according to merit, it is necessary for citizens to know each other, to know what sort of people they are. . . . It is clear then that this is the best way to determine what is a city: as great an excess of population as is needed for self-sufficiency and yet easily taken in at a glance. Let this be our way of defining the size of a city.
>
> Aristotle, *Politics*, VII, 4

The small population meant a homogeneous citizen body. As already noted, citizenship depended upon descent, upon blood relationship, and upon membership in a brotherhood. It was a privilege rarely extended to foreigners. Citizenship gave the right to participate in government to a greater or lesser extent, depending upon the forum. It also meant the privilege and obligation to bear arms and the right to take part in the religious rites of the city. Each state guarded its independence jealously. Rivalry between city-states was intense, and warfare between them chronic.

Sometime during the "dark ages," by about 700 B.C., monarchy of the kind described in the Homeric poems had disappeared, replaced by an aristocracy of large landholders. Later, as a money economy developed, an aristocracy of wealth became dominant in some states. Such government, the rule of the privileged few, is known a *oligarchy*. Oligarchy became more or less permanent in some states and, after most states evolved into democracies, oligarchic factions within those cities persisted.

The rule of aristocrats and oligarchs rested on wealth, including the money to buy arms and horses. Full citizenship rights in fact depended upon the capacity to buy arms. As more men were able to buy arms a new type of citizen-soldier emerged—the hoplite. Hoplites were heavily armed infantry who fought at close quarters in phalanx formation and constituted a formidable new force. The rise of the hoplites marked the decline of the military power of the old aristocrats.

Sometimes tyrants seized power with the aid of hoplite forces, challenging the domination of the aristocrats. Originally the word "tyrant" had no evil connotation to Greeks; it simply meant a person who seized power and overthrew the existing government by extra-legal means. Tyrants, themselves members of the aristocracy, often rose to power by appealing to the common people. Tyranny weakened the hereditary aristocracy and sometimes, as in the case of Athens, paved the way for democracy. In the city-states on the mainland tyranny was usually short-lived, while in Asia Minor and Sicily prolonged tyrannies were more common.

By the fifth century many states had evolved into democracies. The small size of the *polis* and the small homogeneous citizen body made possible direct participation in government, in a system that was in some ways like a New England town meeting. However, conflict between oligarchic factions and democratic factions continued. As one writer has said: "For the Greeks themselves the question whether the whole population or only a privileged section shared in the rule, was one of supreme importance and the most passionate wars" (Ehrenberg, p. 47).

Colonization

Changes in government reflected social and economic changes and unrest. Unrest at home was also a factor in causing another dispersal of population, usually called colonization, from older city-states to new settlements scattered around much of the Mediterranean. Actual settlement was probably preceded by earlier maritime ventures. (The *Odyssey*, for example, gives evidence of considerable knowledge of geography.) Motives for the founding of new settlements were probably mixed. Desire for bases for trade may have played a part. Probably more important was population pressure, which resulted in part from economic distress due to the limited amount of arable land in Greece. Undoubtedly another reason was to relieve pressures on government by disaffected parts of the population. In other words, colonies formed a safety valve which helped to preserve the stability of existing regimes, usually aristocracies. In new settlements colonists could find better land for farming and also the opportunity to raise their status in society.

The earliest movement was westward to the islands and coasts of the Ionian Sea, Sicily, and southern Italy. The first colony was Cumae on the Bay of Naples (c. 750 B.C.). Thereafter so many settlements were made in southern Italy that the Romans called the entire area Magna Graecia. Greek colonies dotted the coast of the eastern two-thirds of Sicily. The most important one was Syracuse, which became for a time the largest and most powerful Greek city-state. There were Greek settlements in southern France. One of them, Massilia, is modern Marseille. Colonies in the west were founded by a number of city-states of which Corinth was the most important.

Some years later colonies were planted in the east. Eventually there were settlements along most of the coast of the Black Sea. Byzantium, which became Constantinople, was founded by Megara. Other important colonies were sent out by Miletus on the Asian coast. In both east and west, settlements which had been themselves originally colonies in turn founded colonies of their own.

The word "colony," as it refers to Greek settlements, does not imply the subordination of the colony to the founding state as, for example, the thirteen American colonies were subordinate to Great Britain. The founding of the Greek colonies was no mere migration to new lands. Colonies were planned, sponsored, and financed by a mother city (*metropolis*) or sometimes a group of older cities. A site was selected after city leaders received the approval of the oracle at Delphi, and a governor and leaders were appointed by the mother city. But once the colony was established it was entirely independent, another sovereign *polis*. It would probably copy the government of the mother city and would share the same gods and religious cults. The colony and mother city might, and often did, have trade and military alliances, but the colony was not subordinate.

Founded primarily as agrarian enterprises, colonies were usually located in areas where farm lands were better and more abundant than in old Greece. Colonization resulted in the multiplication of Greek city-states and in the spread of Greek culture—language, religion, art, drama, and athletic contests. Colonies were founded along the coast. The Greeks did not try to dominate the land of the people of the interior, but the native population along the coast became thoroughly Hellenized.

The founding of these new agricultural settlements meant a source of grain and other food and raw materials for the older Greek cities. In turn they created markets for goods from the older cities and stimulated trade and industry.

Religion

The ancient Greeks believed in the existence of many gods (polytheism), in contrast to the Judeo-Christian concept of one supreme God (monotheism). The Greeks attributed superhuman and supernatural characteristics to many entities and forces. They endowed these forces with personal attributes and thought of them as idealized and magnified human beings. They were portrayed in sculpture and described in literature as having the physical characteristics of human beings (*anthropomorphism*). Like humans, the gods displayed both virtues and vices. They quarreled among themselves, fell in love with human beings, bore grudges against mortals and one another, and took sides in human wars. But they did not cause human suffering. As Zeus is made to say in the *Odyssey:*

> How foolish men are! How unjustly they blame
> the gods! It is their lot to suffer, but
> because of their own folly they bring upon
> themselves sufferings over and above what is
> fated for them. And then they blame the gods.
>
> Book I, Lattimore translation

Even the gods were subject to fate, but the fate of the gods was not the fate of humankind. Humans were mortal, the gods immortal. But Greek religion did not reflect an image of humankind as weak and timid before the gods. Quite the opposite. So near were human beings to the gods, so like them in form and intellect, that a person "had always to be reminding himself that Man is not God, and that it is impious to think it" (Kitto, 61). Thus, the gods punished those who overstepped the bounds.

The mixed ancestry of Greek religion—Minoan and Mycenaean—resulted in inconsistencies and contradictions in myths, legends, and even in the attributes and functions of individual deities. The poems of Homer, which to Greeks had authority similar to that of the Bible for many Christians, brought some order out of this confusion. The poet Hesiod, who lived shortly after Homer, composed a *Theogony* or *Genesis of the Gods*, in which he attempted to systematize some of the myths and create a kind of genealogy of the gods.

The concept of the Divine Family, the principal deities living on Mount Olympus, came primarily from Homer. Here dwelt the king of the gods, Zeus—god of the sky—and Hera, his sharp-tongued wife. Zeus' brother was Poseidon, king of the sea. Athena, virgin goddess of wisdom, and Aphrodite, goddess of love and beauty, were daughters of Zeus. Husband to the lovely Aphrodite was lame Hephaestus, blacksmith to the gods, forger of the great shield of Achilles, and the only Olympian who was not a model of physical perfection. Here too are the twins: Artemis, goddess of the hunt, and her brother Apollo, sun god and god of prophecy. Other dwellers on Olympus included Demeter, earth mother, goddess of the fruits and riches of the fields; and Hermes, wing-sandaled messenger to the gods. Hades, the god of the Underworld and brother to Zeus, did not dwell on Olympus, nor did Dionysus, god of dynamic forces such as the power of sex and wine. Although he was not native to Greece and not a member of the Olympian family, Dionysus was worshipped throughout Greece. In addition to the gods and goddesses recognized by all Greeks, every locality had its own deities, and lesser deities such as river gods were identified with the forces of nature.

Since the gods exercised power over the affairs of humans, people sought to discover the will of the gods and to honor and please them. Religion in this sense pervaded every aspect of Greek family life and the affairs of the *polis*. Almost every function was preceded by a sacrifice. Shrines and altars were everywhere. The greatest architectural achievements of the Greeks were the temples, which were not places of worship like a Hebrew synagogue or a Christian church, but were built to honor a god or goddess. The one best known to us, the Parthenon in Athens, honored Athena. Each temple held a statue of the deity and an altar. Sculptures adorning the temples depicted the gods and religious myths.

The gods, like the Greeks themselves, loved contests, and the religious festivals in their honor were also contests. Greek dramas were written and produced for contests in festivals honoring Dionysus. Games and athletic contests featuring physical prowess also honored the gods. Most famous were the Olympic games, held ever four years at Olympia in honor of Zeus. The first games were believed to have been held in 776 B.C. One of the methods for dating events was by olympiads, the intervals between the games. The main attractions at the games were athletic contests—chariot races, boxing, wrestling. Later the games also included contests in music, poetry, and dancing. Competition was intense. The contests reflected well the values of the aristocrats of the archaic age to whom honor was the greatest virtue, to be striven for even at the cost of one's life. Losing was a crushing dishonor and source of shame.

The games were pan-Hellenic, bringing together participants and spectators from all parts of the Greek world. They were important, along with a common religion and mythology, in making Greeks aware of the distinctive qualities which set them apart from non-Greeks.

Other pan-Hellenic religious institutions, notably the oracles, were sacred places where persons sought to learn the will of the gods. The shrine of Apollo at Delphi was pre-eminent. Here Apollo himself was believed to respond to inquiries. The exact procedures are not clear, but persons who had performed required sacrifices and purification rites were permitted to address themselves to the god, who replied through a priestess (the *Pythia*). Her words were then transcribed by a chief priest. The replies were frequently ambiguous, and the inquirer was left to interpret them. The influence and prestige of Delphi were very great. Greek literature is full of allusions to the prophecies of the oracle, which was consulted on such matters as the founding of a colony and the declaration of war. One famous example is the account by Herodotus of the answer given to King Croesus when he inquired about whether he should attack the Persian army. The oracle replied that if he attacked, a great army would be destroyed, without, of course, telling him that it might be his own army.

The oracle also taught rules of conduct, emphasizing tradition and such virtues as moderation and self-control, which the Greeks thought differentiated them from barbarians. Its lessons are summed up in two often-quoted admonitions: "Know thyself," and "Nothing in excess"; that is, recognize that you are only a human being (not a god), and recognize your limitations. Don't be guilty of excessive pride or arrogance (*hubris*).

Despite emphasis on certain virtues, traditional Greek religion lacked elements considered central to Hebrew, Christian and Islamic faith. It lacked ethical content. The gods themselves were sometimes guilty of conduct which in humans was considered immoral. Emphasis was on ritual rather than theology. There was no body of sacred authoritative literature like the Bible and the Quran. Priests and priestesses at shrines and temples performed specific rituals and sacrifices, but they did not teach doctrine or preach right conduct. Just as no god represented supreme good, neither was there a deity of absolute evil.

The promise of immortality and personal salvation, so important in Christian thought, was largely absent from Greek religion. Ideas about afterlife were nebulous and seldom mentioned. When Odysseus in the Eleventh Book of the *Odyssey* visits the realm of Hades, the Underworld, he encounters shades of the dead who lead a ghostly and cheerless existence. The shade of Achilles, hero of the *Iliad*, sums up the Greek view of afterlife:

Let me hear no smooth talk of death from you, Odysseus, light
   of councils.
Better, I say, to break sod as a farm hand
for some poor country man, on iron rations,
than lord it over all the exhausted dead.

                                        Robert Fitzgerald translation

For a few, mystery cults offered promise of salvation. These
cults were usually associated with Demeter and Dionysus, deities of the birth and rebirth of vegetation. Most famous were the
Eleusinian Mysteries at the shrine of Demeter at Eleusis near
Athens. From the belief that Demeter gave fertility to the fields
developed the belief that she could give immortality to the human soul. The cult was secret, open only to the initiated; conse-
quently few details are known. Members were required to go
through purification rites and other rituals. Those who were initiated were promised future salvation.

This way to salvation was largely a matter of ritual. The
Judeo-Christian concept of a code of ethical behavior and a personal God who forgave sin was lacking in Greek thought. Greeks
found no hope of forgiveness for their sins or mistakes in their
religion. But Greek religion was no barrier to human progress. It
may, in fact, have had a liberating effect. The fact that the gods
were so like humans and were not omnipotent reduced fear of
them and left room for human reason and initiative. The very
"emptiness" of Greek religion caused the Greeks to seek answers
to the riddles of life and human behavior through philosophical
and scientific speculation. In the fifth and fourth centuries skepticism about the traditional gods grew. Some philosophers appeared to be moving toward monotheism. But Greek culture of
the classical era was primarily humanistic and secular.

Archaic Literature and Art

In the archaic period as Greeks became more aware of their
common heritage—their language, religion, and other institutions—the concept of Hellenism developed. Greeks did not consider themselves a chosen people as did the Hebrews, but they
considered themselves culturally unique and superior. One
thing that distinguished them from other people was their lan-

guage. They thought that persons who did not speak Greek could not think like Greeks. Hence non-Greeks were barbarians. Greeks also considered their form of government, the *polis*, evidence of their superiority. Persons under other forms of government could not be truly free as were Greeks. This feeling of superiority, inconsistent with modern American ideals of cultural pluralism, was exhilarating and probably contributed to the originality and artistic creativity of the archaic years.

During this period there was a shift from epic poetry, the stories of great heroes and great deeds, to a more personal kind of expression, the lyric. One of the most gifted of the poets was Sappho of the island of Lesbos, the only woman who appears to have won wide acclaim in the history of Greek literature. Sappho writes of the private emotions: of love, and loneliness and vulnerability. Later poetry, while retaining a personal quality, was often written in celebration of public events—religious games and festivals.

Beginning in the seventh century, stone temples replaced wooden structures. Most of these have disappeared, destroyed in war or demolished to make way for later buildings. Some fine examples survive, however, in the Greek west, notably at Paestum (the Greek colony of Poseidonia) in southern Italy. The sculptures which adorn these temples, designed to honor the gods, also reflect a growing interest in the human being, in the representation of the human figure. While the statues of the archaic period still show some of the stylized rigidity of earlier forms (facial expressions, for example, seem always to be frozen into what has become known as the "archaic smile"), the form of the body is fuller and more relaxed. Retaining the strength of earlier forms, the statues of archaic times are more detailed, warmer and more vigorous. They clearly foreshadow the culmination of artistic achievement of the fifth and fourth centuries.

Vase painting developed in this period along the same lines—that is, away from the rigidly formalized and toward softer, more human renditions. Decorators replaced the geometric style of earlier years with scenes from religious myths and everyday life. Beyond their artistic value, Greek vases are important documents for the student of Greek history. The detail of the vases illustrates and supplements the literary record.

Beginnings of Philosophy and Science

Perhaps the most enduring and profound legacy of ancient Greece was philosophy. A conspicuous and important characteristic of the Greeks was their rationalism—their belief that they could solve problems by human reason—and their spirit of inquiry. They questioned both the nature of the physical world and the nature of humankind and went beyond experience to ask about causes. Whence the gods? they asked. And whence ourselves? Where are the winds and why do they blow? And later: what is virtue and how can it be achieved? Where is happiness?

Earlier Greeks had found answers in mythology and the supernatural. These answers are typically specific and unique, providing no general explanation. Thunder occurred, for example, when Zeus, for some particular reason, was angry and threw his bolts across the sky. The great contribution of the Greeks, beginning in the archaic period, was that they sought general answers through rational inquiry.

Philosophy, literally "love of wisdom," originated in Ionia on the coast of Asia Minor in the sixth century B.C. The first important figure was Thales of Miletus. A few years later a second school of philosophy, named after its founder, Pythagoras, arose in southern Italy. These early thinkers were cosmologists, students of the cosmos, of the basic nature of the universe. Thales and his followers found first principles in matter. The Pythagoreans sought the primary cause of all things—the harmonious movement of the stars for example—in numbers. The mathematical investigations of the Pythagoreans gave impetus not only to exactitude in science but also to the larger concept that the universe is a reasonable place, based upon mathematical constants (not chance) and thus discoverable by human reason.

The Greeks did not distinguish between philosophy and science as do we. Indeed, they had no word for the category of knowledge we call science. Thales is regarded as the founder of Greek scientific inquiry as well as philosophy.

The theories of these early thinkers were speculative, often empirically inaccurate. Most important for the development of rational inquiry as the basis for western civilization was that they braved the questions, opening a new era in human thought, free from the supernatural and from religious mysticism.

Athens and Sparta

By far the largest and most powerful of the city-states and the ones about which we know most were Athens and Sparta. They dominated the history of the Greeks for almost two hundred years after 500 B.C. Their institutions furnish a lively and illuminating study in contrasting change based on a common tradition.

Sparta and Spartan Institutions

Sparta was the name of the city-state which embraced the entire geographical region in the Peloponnesus called Laconia. Inhabitants were known to the Greeks as Lacedaemonians. Sometime in the eighth century Sparta conquered the neighboring territory of Messenia, thereby acquiring more land and laborers. The land was distributed among the Spartan citizens. Probably because of the conquest of Messenia, Sparta did not found colonies to relieve population pressure as other Greek states were doing in that period. The Messenians endured their lot for some generations, but about 650 B.C. it appears that they revolted against Spartan domination. The Messenian revolt underscored the precarious position of the Spartan citizen body, which was a small minority ruling over an oppressed majority. This basic fact probably accounted for the unique, regimented, militaristic regime of Sparta in historic times.

Tradition attributed the peculiar nature of the Spartan system to a legendary law-giver by the name of Lycurgus. In reality the system probably evolved over a period of time, with the Messenian revolt giving a final impetus to some features. Before the Messenian revolt Sparta appears to have followed a pattern similar to that of other Greek states. For example there were Spartan poets before that date. But after 600 B.C. not a single Spartan is known as a writer or for any other cultural or artistic activity.

There were three classes of population in Sparta. At the top were the Spartan citizens, a small minority. The possession of abundant land for agriculture and a large body of forced labor made it possible for Spartan citizens to devote most of their time to military pursuits. Labor was provided by a group know as *helots*, who comprised the majority of the population. These helots were like serfs, bound to the land of their Spartan masters. The origins of this class are obscure. They do not appear to have been of different stock or language from Spartan citizens. After the conquest of Messenia its inhabitants were reduced to the condition of helots of the Spartans. The third population group was called *perioikoi*, literally "dwellers around." They were not helots but they did not possess the rights of citizenship. They lived on the fringes of Laconia and carried on necessary trade and commerce. They were subject to military service in times of crisis.

The governmental structure of Sparta retained some of the characteristics of Homeric monarchy but also had some distinctive features. Rather than one king, Sparta had two kings and two royal families. The origins of the dual kingship are not known. The two kings were commanders-in-chief of Spartan armies. There was also a council of elders, the *gerousia*, consisting of twenty-eight members, all of them men of more than sixty years of age, chosen from old aristocratic families. The council exercised important powers in advising the kings and in preparing legislation.

An assembly of all male citizens over thirty years of age had the power to declare war and to vote on matters prepared by the council. In contrast to the Athenian assembly, which could amend measures presented by the council and which was noted for prolonged debate and eloquent oratory, the Spartan assembly could only approve or disapprove a measure brought before it. There was no debate. Spartans were known as people of few words; hence our adjective "laconic." In addition to the kings and council there were five magistrates known as *ephors* who exercised general supervisory powers and in some ways acted as a check on the powers of the kings.

The entire Spartan citizen body was a professional army in contrast to the other Greek states which relied on citizen militia. The whole social system—marriage, family life, education—was geared to produce brave, disciplined soldiers and to maintain military preparedness. The state had the authority to order that weak or disabled children be exposed to the elements immediately after birth. A boy was in the care of his mother until he reached the age of seven, when he was placed directly under the control of the state. Thereafter he was trained in athletics and military drill and endurance of physical dangers and discomforts. At the age of twenty the young man became liable to service in the field. He was allowed to marry but not to have what we would consider a normal home life. He spent most of his life in military barracks with other soldiers. Hunting, riding, and athletic contests were his recreation.

Spartan girls were also trained for physical fitness. After marriage, while their husbands spent most of their time in the military, wives had comparative freedom and comfort as well as responsibility for the management of property. Spartan women enjoyed a status and liberty superior to that of their homebound Athenian sisters.

The militaristic nature of Spartan government and society arose partly out of fear of helot revolt. Spartans constantly lived in fear of subversion and uprisings. For these reasons Sparta preferred not to be drawn too far away from home in military and diplomatic ventures, though she did ally herself with other city-states, mostly in the Peloponnesus in an arrangement that is usually known as the Peloponnesian League. Sparta was the "hegemon" or leader of the Peloponnesian League. Sparta was obligated to protect her allies in time of war and they were obligated to follow her lead.

Spartan military discipline and power made her a formidable foe and became legendary. Sparta's role in the Persian Wars was vital to the survival of Greek freedom. Her citizens were the best soldiers of the age and did not lose a battle until 371 B.C. Because she presented an image of conservatism and stability in contrast to the constant shifts in power and policies of many Greek states, Sparta was an object of admiration by certain philosophers who tended to idealize her institutions.

But Sparta was betrayed by the very strength of her system, a lopsided strength in which emphasis on military preparedness retarded development along other lines. In fact Spartan citizens were forbidden to travel. They were suspicious of new ideas, and their training did not prepare them to deal with new situations. Although Sparta defeated Athens in the Peloponnesian War, she proved incapable of governing an empire after her victory.

Athens Before 500 B.C.

Athens was a more typical Greek state than was Sparta. Her territory and population were much larger but in other respects her development and institutions were similar to those of most Greek states.

Sometime before 750 B.C. Athens had absorbed the whole of Attica. The process was apparently peaceful. Athenian citizenship was extended to all the free male population of Attica, but citizens had to come to the city of Athens to exercise their political rights. The expansion over Attica appears to have occurred under the rule of kings. About 750 B.C. the monarchy was replaced by aristocracy, the powers of the king distributed among three magistrates known as *archons*. A council of nobles (later known as the *areopagus*) was the real center of power. There was also an *ecclesia* or assembly of all male citizens, but in early times its functions were limited to approval or disapproval of acts of the council.

Under the rule of the aristocrats the less privileged classes were subject to exploitation, in part because the law, based on oral tradition and custom, had long been the monopoly of the ruling class. One of the first reforms won by the lower classes was codification of the laws. In Athens the famous "law giver" was Solon, who was given extraordinary power in the face of a threat of civil war which grew out of unrest among oppressed small farmers. Many farmers were losing farms to creditors, and some, although they were Athenian citizens, were sold into slavery because of debts.

One of the most important reforms of Solon was abolition of enslavement for debt. The guarantee of a free citizen body was the foundation for the development of Athenian democracy. One of the reforms in government was classification of the citizen body on a property basis (a classification used earlier for military purposes), thereby reducing the power of the hereditary aristocrats and opening the way for new leaders.

These and other reforms of Solon did not end strife between the classes. The power of the aristocracy was not broken, nor were the problems of the poorest class—who wanted land distribution, in addition to abolition of enslavement for debt and cancellation of mortgages—dealt with adequately. This situation paved the way for the tyranny of Peisistratus, who came to power about 540 B.C. Although Peisistratus was a "tyrant"—that is, one who seizes power by extra-legal methods—his rule was not oppressive. Though an aristocrat himself, Peisistratus broke the power of the old aristocracy, sending some members into exile, and distributing their land to small farmers. The prosperity and power of Athens increased under his rule. He sought to make Athens the cultural center of Hellas. After the death of Peisistratus his two sons ruled for a few years, but the tyranny was overthrown in 510 B.C.

After the tyranny the most powerful figure in Athens was Cleisthenes, the leader of the *demos* or popular party (as distinguished from the aristocratic or oligarchic party). Like most leaders of the *demos*, Cleisthenes was a member of an aristocratic family. Under his leadership reforms were carried out which reduced sectional and class strife and extended full political rights to all male citizens except those of the poorest class. The citizen body was divided into ten tribes in which membership depended on residence, not ancestry. A new Council of Five Hundred, consisting of fifty men from each tribe, was created and became the real center of power in the government. But all citizens participated in the assembly, which debated and passed legislation prepared by the council and elected the principal magistrates. Then elected *strategoi* (generals), one from each tribe, commanded tribal regiments and formed a council of war. They were not professional military officers. Certain of these elected *strategoi* soon became the most influential political figures and most powerful officials of the state.

By the beginning of the fifth century Athens had developed an almost completely democratic system of government. Soon afterward the war with the Persians, the greatest challenge the people of Hellas had faced, led to the complete democratization of the constitution.

PART II

THE FIFTH CENTURY: A SURVEY

The years between 500 B.C. and 400 B.C., which encompass the most brilliant era in Greek art and literature, began with the Persian Wars, in which the Greeks united to repulse the armies of the mighty Persian Empire. The century ended in the prolonged conflict among the Greeks themselves, known as the Peloponnesian War, in which the two leading states, Athens and Sparta, and their allies struggled for supremacy. Sparta was ultimately victorious and Athens exhausted and defeated. The aspects of Greek civilization in the fifth century which concern us in Change and Tradition can be better understood against a background of the important military and political developments.

The Persian Wars

It is difficult to imagine two societies and systems of government more dissimilar than the tiny Greek city-states and the vast Persian Empire. The Persians, hitherto an obscure tribe centered in what is today Iran, broke up the mighty Assyrian Empire and expanded their power until, during the reign of Cyrus the Great (559-527 B.C.), they ruled over an empire which stretched from the shores of the Aegean Sea to India. Egypt was added by Cambyses, the son of Cyrus.

The Persian Empire was a mixture of diverse peoples and cultures—Persians, Egyptians, Indians, Jews, Phoenicians, and some Greeks from the cities along the coast of Asia Minor. A highly developed administrative system evolved under Cyrus. Persian rule over the conquered people was usually not oppressive, but all subjects were required to pay tribute and to perform military service.

The mainland Greeks probably viewed the expansion of the Persians and their absorption of Lydia and the Greek cities in Asia Minor within its borders with some apprehension, but at first they took no action. The revolt of some of the Greek cities of Ionia in 499 B.C. led Athens to send naval and military aid. The Persians ruthlessly crushed the rebellion, and the people of Miletus, who had led the revolt, were put to death or enslaved, an action which frightened and appalled Greeks everywhere.

Apparently out of a desire to retaliate against the Athenians for their interference and to intimidate them, the Persian king, Darius, sent a small expeditionary force by sea. The Persian ships landed on the east coast of Attica near the plain of Marathon. Attacking by surprise, an army of Athenians and a few allies from Plataea routed the Persians in hand-to-hand fighting. Although it was a relatively small engagement, the victory at Marathon gave the Athenians confidence to make preparations to resist if the Persians returned. It was widely expected that another Persian attack to avenge their defeat was inevitable.

In the years following Marathon, Themistocles, leader of the democratic faction, emerged as the strong man in Athenian politics and the leader who devised the strategy which enabled a united Hellas to defeat the Persians. Convinced that success against the Persians and the future of Greece lay in the development of a strong Athenian navy, he insisted that revenues from the state-owned silver mines should be used to build a fleet. Well-to-do Athenians also contributed money to build ships. By 480 B.C. Athens had a fleet of at least 200 vessels. In addition her allies contributed perhaps a hundred ships. These wooden ships, tiny and fragile, were manned by sailors from the poorer class of Athenians who could not afford to buy heavy arms required to serve in the hoplite forces. The basic strategy was to maneuver the ship into close quarters with an enemy vessel and ram up against it if possible, breaking its oars. The heavily armed infantry from the Greek vessel then boarded the ship and engaged in hand-to-hand fighting.

Meanwhile the Persians made elaborate preparations for an invasion of Greece by land and sea. This time they planned a march by land across the Hellespont (the straits between Europe and Asia Minor) which was crossed by a pontoon bridge, and down the eastern coast of the Greek mainland. Naval units were to accompany the land forces and supply them. Figures given by the historian Herodotus are clearly too large, but the Persian forces were much larger than the Greek. As the mighty Persian army advanced, many Greek cities on the islands and along the coast responded to threats and sometimes bribery by capitulating to the Persians without fighting.

The two most powerful Greek states, however—Athens and Sparta—decided to resist. For once they presented a united front and rallied allies from among the other Greeks to form a Hellenic League. Sparta was given command of the land forces, but the basic strategy was planned by Themistocles. The hope of stopping the Persian advance by fighting at easily defensible points was shattered when a small Spartan army, which fought to the last man, was destroyed at Thermopylae.

As the Persian army advanced, most of the population of Athens was evacuated to the island of Salamis off the coast. The Persians then entered Athens and pillaged it. The Spartans were building fortifications at the isthmus of Corinth, hoping to stop an invasion of the Peloponnesus, but Themistocles insisted upon fighting a naval battle off the coast near Athens. At Salamis in 480 B.C. small and more maneuverable Athenian ships won a decisive victory over the Persian fleet. Thereafter the Persian king Xerxes withdrew most of the remainder of his fleet, leaving behind a large land force. The following year a Spartan army defeated these troops at Plataea in Boeotia. The Persian commander was killed and the Persians withdrew to Asia.

The Athenian Empire

Greece had been saved. The effects were exhilarating, particularly in Athens. The victory over the Persians led to the complete democratization of the Athenian government. The battle of Salamis had been won through the efforts of the sailors, members of the *thetes,* the poorest class of Athenians. They were now given full political rights.

Although the Persian invaders had been driven out, no formal treaty ended the war. Many Greek cities on the islands and the Asian coast were still under Persian rule, and there was no guarantee that the Persians would not attempt another invasion of the mainland.

Sparta emerged from the war with a strong army. She had not been invaded and devastated as Athens had been. She was not a naval power, however, and because of her chronic fear of uprising at home she tended to follow an isolationist course. Thus, it was natural that Greek cities would look to Athens for leadership and protection. After the war Athens and her allies formed the Delian League, called by that name because the treasury was on the island of Delos. The purpose of the alliance was to defend members against renewed attack by the Persians and to free the Greek states still under Persian rule. All members furnished ships or money for the common purpose. Athens, by far the strongest member, furnished the leadership, and although she was not assessed as other members were, she furnished far more ships to the navy than any other member. Ships were built in Athens and the crews recruited there.

In the next few years as the result of victories by the Athenian fleet, most of the Greek cities were liberated and the Persian threat ended. Athens was the dominant power in the Aegean area. The purposes of the Delian League achieved, some of the allies wanted to withdraw. But Athens was unwilling to dissolve the alliance and forced cities which tried to leave to sign new treaties and to pay tribute to Athens. Ultimately all the allies but three were made subjects. They were required to pay tribute to Athens and often to adopt constitutions similar to the Athenian constitution, which favored the *demos* or popular party. In these states an oligarchic party usually opposed Athenian domination. The money collected from the members was used in part to pay for a navy which protected them, but some of the surplus was used to rebuild and beautify Athens. The treasury was moved from Delos to Athens. This aggressive, imperialistic foreign policy, which reached its peak under Pericles, was strongly supported by the democratic faction in Athens, and especially by the sailors and groups which benefited from the commerce which accompanied Athens' expanding naval power.

Thus the Delian League became the Athenian Empire, which rested on the strength of the Athenian navy. The rule of Athens was defended by the assertion that Athens ruled justly and that members were more secure and better off than they would have been outside the empire. In the Funeral Oration of Pericles, as remembered by Thucydides, Pericles claimed: "No subject claims that Athens is an unworthy master." It is true that many cities grew and flourished in the period of Athenian domination, but Athens failed to develop any method by which members were represented in decision making. Other city-states viewed the empire as violating the basic Greek ideals of autonomy and freedom.

The Peloponnesian War

Almost as soon as the Persians were driven from the mainland, relations between the two great powers of the Greek world, Athens and Sparta, began to deteriorate. Sparta at first hoped to keep Athens, which had suffered from the war, militarily weak, and as the latter's empire grew, Sparta became apprehensive.

Eventually the two former allies were drawn into conflict with each other. Thucydides, the great historian who lived through the events of the war, has left us a fascinating study of the complexity of the causes, remote and underlying as well as immediate and specific, which triggered the outbreak of hostilities. He also shows the difficulties of determining war guilt: Sparta blamed Athens; Athens, Sparta. Thucydides decided that the fundamental cause of the war was growing fear of Athenian power throughout Hellas.

The war, which involved much of the Greek world including Sicily in the later stages, began in 431 B.C. when a Spartan army invaded Attica. Pericles, the Athenian leader, was optimistic about the outcome because he believed that Sparta would be unable to sustain a long war against superior Athenian resources. He outlined a strategy for Athens: to fight a defensive war, to conserve manpower, and to avoid risks. Because of her navy and access to the sea, Athens could endure a long war even if Attica itself was invaded. Pericles warned against trying to enlarge the empire while Athens was at war. "I am more afraid of our own blunders," he said, "than of the enemy's devices."

Pericles' strategy, although basically sound, failed to take into account an unexpected natural disaster which struck during the second year of the war. When the Spartans began their annual invasion and much of the population of Attica was crowded within the city walls of Athens for protection, the plague, beginning in the east, reached the Athenian port of Pireaus and spread rapidly within the city. It is estimated that as much as a third of the population died during the epidemic, and the survivors were demoralized. Pericles himself died in 429 B.C.

After the death of Pericles no leader of comparable stature emerged to command public confidence and to assure continuity of policy. Nevertheless for a number of years Athens continued to win victories, but they were not decisive. In 421 B.C. the Peace of Nicias was negotiated between Athens and Sparta. It was intended to last for fifty years, but neither side was willing to observe the provisions, and the war was renewed. As the war dragged on, Athens' allies began to defect and the new Athenian leadership took ruthless measures to prevent them from withdrawing from the empire. There were also attempts to compel cities which sought to remain neutral into the Athenian empire. Most notorious was the example of the island of Melos, which refused to yield to Athens' demands and whose inhabitants were slaughtered or sold into slavery in reprisal. In relating this and other episodes in the war, Thucydides gives us an illuminating account of the forces released by war which turned the hitherto humane and moderate Athenians to ruthless brutality.

The most disastrous venture of the Athenians was the Sicilian expedition, a resumption of the policy of imperial expansion against which Pericles had warned. Using as a pretext a request for aid by one of the smaller Greek colonies on the island, the Athenian expedition laid siege to Syracuse, the most powerful city in the west. From the beginning the Athenian forces suffered from weak and divided leadership. In the face of losses, instead of giving up the effort and ordering a withdrawal the Athenian assembly voted to send reinforcements, but the Spartans also sent a fleet to aid Syracuse. Thucydides' narration of the defeat of the navel forces in Syracuse harbor, the retreat overland, and the final annihilation of the Athenian forces which had sailed from Athens with such high hopes has the power of a Greek tragedy.

The Sicilian disaster led to a short-lived oligarchic regime in Athens, but the Athenians remained resilient in spite of defeats and dwindling resources. They won some brilliant victories and refused to make peace. Finally their last fleet, taken by surprise, was destroyed and the troops massacred. Thereafter the city of Athens was besieged by land and sea and forced to surrender and accept peace terms dictated by Sparta (404 B.C.). Athens lost her empire and her allies. She was allowed to retain only a few naval vessels for police purposes and was compelled to destroy the fortifications which connected the city with the port of Piraeus, and to become an ally of Sparta.

The disastrous end of the war caused the democracy to be discredited, and under Spartan influence and protection an oligarchic government was installed. This regime, called by the Athenians the Thirty Tyrants, instituted a reign of terror, including political executions, wholesale banishments, and confiscation of property. However, it lasted only a short time. A counter-revolution in 403 led to the restoration of the democracy. Athens never regained the power she had possessed before the war, but she continued to be the cultural center of Hellas.

SOCIETY AND ECONOMY
IN FIFTH CENTURY ATHENS

It is difficult for a twentieth century American to imagine how the people of ancient Athens actually lived. Although Athens was by far the most populous and wealthy of the Greek city-states, by our standards the life-style of the inhabitants was extremely simple, even primitive. The fifth century was a period of intense intellectual ferment and creativity, but the energies and resources of Athenians were not directed toward enhancing physical comfort and convenience. Perhaps the most striking difference between ancient Athens and modern America is the absence of machinery and technology and interest in material progress.

There are no accurate statistics about the size of the population, and all estimates are speculative. Unlike the ancient Chinese and Romans, the Greeks did not take censuses. Most of the population lived in the urban center, the site of the modern city of Athens. Houses of mud brick, originally clustered together for security reasons, continued to be built on narrow streets. The exteriors were plain, and life centered on interior courtyards. In larger houses there were separate women's quarters. With rare exceptions even the wealthiest Athenians lived simply and did not display their wealth through luxurious houses and ostentatious living. Because of the mild climate all Greek men led an outdoors life. The Agora, a large square surrounded by colonnades, was the center of civic life. Here were located public buildings, and here men came to do business and congregate and meet friends.

Although Athens was the most urban of Greek states, a large part of the population continued to be rural and to make a living from agriculture. Probably a majority of citizens in the fifth century owned land, often tiny plots. They continued to live in the city of Athens or surrounding villages and work in the countryside. Methods of farming were primitive and unchanging for the most part, but more progressive farmers turned to raising olives and viniculture. Olive oil and wine were important export commodities. The rocky soil of Attica did not produce enough grain to meet the needs of the city and importation of grain was vital to the survival of Athens.

Industry in the sense of factories and machinery simply did not exist. There were workshops in which artisans—both free and slave—made such articles as shoes, metal utensils, and armor. Many necessities such as cloth were largely produced in the home.

Overseas trade was important to the economy. As we have seen, Athenian imperialism was motivated in part by the desire to control trade and trade routes. Shipbuilding was an important occupation, furnishing employment to many inhabitants. The elite of Athens continued to be the landholding aristocracy, but commerce was the most important means of amassing wealth.

There were three distinct classes of residents: citizens, resident foreigners (*metics*) who were usually fellow Greeks from other city-states, and slaves. As we have already seen, the Greek concept of citizenship was exclusive. In fifth century Athens citizenship—the right to participate in the government and many activities of the *polis*—was a right based on birth. The center of society was the family (*oikos*). Families were grouped into brotherhoods (*phratries*), and citizenship was only only to persons who were members of a phratry. At some earlier periods citizenship was extended to certain groups such as men who fought on the side of Athens during a war or who had performed other meritorious services, but a law passed in 451 B.C. made the requirements more restrictive. The new law, passed at a time when large numbers of non-Athenian Greeks were flocking to the city because of the empire and economic opportunities, stipulated that only persons both of whose parents were Athenian citizens were citizens. Thus, the child of an Athenian citizen married to a metic woman was not a citizen.

There was a large class of metics, probably at least as large as the citizen body. They chose to live in Athens because of the economic opportunities offered by Athenian commerce. They were not an oppressed group, but they did not possess the right to participate in the government of the *polis*. They were protected by Athenian law, and in return were obligated to military service and financial support of the state.

Finally there was a large slave population. The institution of slavery—i.e. buying and selling and owning human beings—was common to all ancient civilizations. It did not occur to the average Athenian to question the morality of the institution. Enslavement was not based on race as it was in the United States and Latin America at a later time. Indeed Greeks were sometimes enslaved by other Greeks. Captives taken in war were one source of slaves. Other slaves came from the slave markets of the Near East or were kidnapped from among peoples living along the coast of the Black Sea. Phoenician traders carried slaves from one end of the Mediterranean to the other. In the fifth century a majority of the slaves in Athens were probably non-Greek.

Except that slaves were property and their status hereditary, Athenian slavery bore little resemblance to plantation slavery in the United States. Some slaves were agricultural workers, but farms were small. Other slaves performed domestic service. Many were skilled artisans who worked alongside free laborers. An inscription found on the Erectheum on the acropolis records the labor force engaged in the construction of the building—twenty-two citizens, forty-two metics, and twenty slaves. All of them were paid the same wages. The wages of the slaves who worked on the Erectheum went to their masters, but slaves could earn their own money in their free time and were sometimes able to buy their freedom. Sometimes slaves were emancipated by their masters. They wore no distinctive clothing or other identifying marks, and they were able to engage in almost all activities except military and political. The one exception to the generally non-oppressive treatment of slaves was the condition of those who worked in stone quarries and mines, and in particular the silver mines at Laurion. Their labors were of a kind that no free Athenian would perform, and they worked under the most degrading conditions.

The existence of a large slave population helped ensure to Athenian citizens the leisure necessary for participation in the time-consuming activities related to the *polis*. Although Greek slavery in Athens and elsewhere was not cruel or oppressive compared with many systems, it nevertheless remains the great paradox of Greek civilization. Athens, which considered itself a symbol of freedom to the rest of the world, had more slaves than any other Greek state.

Each of the above classes included women, of course, but of particular interest to us are the women of the citizen class, members of the Athenian *polis*. Evidence about these women is limited and fragmentary and sometimes contradictory. All of the literary records which survive were written by men, most of whom gave little thought to the status of women. Prose writers—historians, philosophers, orators—and surviving laws depict women almost as non-entities without any legal rights. On the other hand, drama, in which women often play prominent and authoritative roles, gives a somewhat different picture. However, the advice which Pericles gave to women in Thucydides' account appears to sum up what was generally regarded as fitting feminine conduct. After extolling the bravery of the husbands lost in the Peloponnesian War, Pericles addresses the women:

> Perhaps I should say a word or two on the duties of women to those among you who are now widowed. I can say all I have to say in a short word of advice. Your great glory is not to be inferior to what God has made you, and the greatest glory of a woman is to be least talked about by men, whether they are praising you or criticizing you.
>
> Thucydides , 151

Fifth century Athens has been compared to a men's club from which outsiders—metics, slaves, and women—were excluded. As the *polis* became more democratized and the average male citizen more and more involved in public affairs, the lives of women of the citizen class were increasingly restricted and secluded. In the earlier periods women had been more active participants. In the archaic era there was not only Sappho but other women poets as well.

Traditionally, female children were regarded as more of a burden than a blessing. Female infants were more likely to be exposed than were males. This practice, which was seldom mentioned but which nevertheless existed, gave the father the authority to decide whether an infant should survive. Those who were exposed might die or might be raised as foundlings who became slaves. If the daughter survived, the father was obligated to provide dowry before she could marry, and marriage was the only possible life for her.

Legally speaking the status of females was like that of minor children. Before marriage a daughter was entirely subject to her father, after marriage to her husband. She had no voice in the selection of her husband. Girls were married when they were only fourteen or fifteen years old to men often twice their age. Their role in life was determined primarily by their reproductive function. The survival of the *oikos* depended upon male heirs. If a girl married and bore her husband a son she was a respected member of the family and society. If she failed in this function her life was scarcely worth living.

In addition to bearing and nurturing children women performed important domestic work. They made valuable economic contributions, particularly in spinning and weaving cloth. Women's lives were confined entirely to the home and, except for husbands and sons, to members of their own sex. Wives did not join their husbands in entertaining guests. Respectable women were not seen at social events such as dinners.

Of course there were differences between the lives of women of the wealthier classes and women of humbler circumstances. For economic reasons, the lives of poor women were less restricted. Although women of the upper classes seldom appeared outside their houses, women of the poorer classes, lacking slaves, were compelled to perform some tasks outside, such as going to the community well for water. Wives and daughters of farmers worked in the fields and orchards.

Respectable upper-class women appeared in public only in connection with religious events. Women of the citizen class, excluded from political life, participated in a variety of religious activities. In the home they took part in such family rites as marriages and funerals and household sacrifices to the gods. Publicly they participated in religious festivals and processions, but it is not clear whether women attended performances at dramatic festivals. The only public office a woman could hold was that of priestess. Evidence exists of priestesses at a number of sanctuaries in Athens, but their functions are not clear.

It seems obvious that wives educated only in household tasks, married when they were in their early teens, and confined to lives within the house, could furnish little companionship for husbands who spent most of their time away from home and whose chief interests were in public affairs. Nor is it surprising that such men sought female companionship outside the home. There were, of course, common prostitutes, but wealthier, educated men, including Pericles himself, sometimes formed more or less lasting liaisons with women know as *hetairai* (singular *hetaira*). These were metics, more cultivated and free to lead less restricted lives than women of the citizen class.

In a society so strongly masculine men, of course, spent most of their time with others of their own sex. It was regarded as quite natural for older men to form close relationships—sometimes sexual—with youths.

THE ATHENIAN *POLIS*
IN THE AGE OF PERICLES

Ancient Greeks valued freedom, but it was freedom of the individual within the bounds of the family and the *polis*, which was the aggregate of families. The individual's obligations were to family and to the *polis*, and sometimes the two conflicted. One writer says: "Perhaps the most overriding characteristic of the Greek cities was the pressure which they exerted upon the individual citizen to merge his life and interest in those of the group" (Pollitt, 10).

Nowhere was this so true as in Athens. If we are to believe contemporary literature, to Athenian citizens of the fifth century affairs of the *polis* were paramount over other interests. More than wealth, the average citizen wanted leisure enough to participate in public affairs. In the words of Pericles in the Funeral Oration:

> Here each individual is interested not only in his own affairs but in the affairs of the state as well: even those who are mostly occupied with their own business are extremely well-informed on general politics—this is a peculiarity of ours: we do not say that a man who takes no interest in politics is a man who minds his own business; we say that he has no business here at all.
>
> Thucydides , 147

Athens was unlike any modern state in the degree to which the entire citizen body participated in making government policies and in administering them. It is necessary to understand that the supreme authority was the sovereign people themselves (the citizens). There was no supreme law such as the United States Constitution to which to appeal.

The Persian War had led to complete democratization, which meant the removal of all property requirements for participation in government and the beginning of paid participation. The first payments went to those serving in the law courts, enabling workers to take time from regular employment. Later, pay was extended to all kinds of public service. Thus the well-to-do no longer had a monopoly on government.

But the most radical and innovative change and the principal device for insuring the sovereignty of the people was the practice of choosing officials by lot. This began early in the fifth century and was extended to almost all offices. Many details of the procedures are unclear, but the use of the lot (sortition) was intended to prevent any one person from becoming too powerful, to prevent tampering with elections, and to spread responsibilities. Some persons were excluded, such as those convicted of crime or failure to perform military service. Terms of office were short—one or two years—and the number of terms one individual could serve was limited. These procedures ensured that over a period of years almost all citizens had experience in several aspects of government. At the end of every year every official was required to submit to a strict scrutiny and possible prosecution for maladministration.

This was a system of government by amateurs. It was not government by "professionals" or "experts" and was not intended to be. A fifth century document by an unknown author who is usually called "The Old Oligarch" because he was not sympathetic to democracy in principle, nevertheless admitted:

> What it comes to therefore is that a state founded upon such institutions will not be the best state; but, given a democracy, these are the right means to secure its preservation. The People, it must be borne in mind, does not demand that the city be well governed and itself a slave. It desires to be free and to be master. As to bad legislation, it does not concern itself about that.

Robinson, 23

The supreme power lay in the assembly (*ecclesia*), which met four times a month. All citizens were entitled to attend and participate. Meetings were held in the huge outdoor theater of Dionysus. Of course not all citizens ever attended at one time, and attendance fluctuated. The assembly was the body which passed laws and decrees and determined over-all policy, such as declaration of war. Measures for action by the assembly were prepared by the council but could be amended and freely debated before being voted on. There was no authority higher than the assembly and no veto of its acts.

The Council of Five Hundred consisted of fifty representatives from each of the ten tribes into which the citizens were divided. Legislation to be acted upon by the assembly was prepared in the council. It also had control over the administration of policy as determined by the assembly. To carry out day-to-day supervision of administration the council was divided into ten standing committees, each of which served one tenth of the year. All administrative work was carried out by committees of representatives from each tribe. They supervised such matters as public works, building of ships, importation of grain, and the business of the empire. Routine clerical work was often done by slaves.

The one significant exception to selection by lot was the ten *strategoi* or generals, one from each tribe, who were elected by vote of the assembly for a term of one year and were eligible for reelection. Pericles, the greatest statesman of the fifth century, was reelected about thirty times. Nicias, the unfortunate commander of the Sicilian expedition, was elected fourteen times. The *strategoi* sometimes commanded military expeditions but they were not professional military men, and their functions were not primarily military. They were political leaders, usually effective orators, who won the support of the assembly and led in the shaping of policy.

Pericles, like many other *strategoi,* was an aristocrat who firmly believed in the democracy. He inspired public confidence by his good judgment, disinterestedness, and moderation. During the years of his ascendancy he won the trust and devotion of the citizenry as no other leader ever did and had almost unchallenged authority during the years when the power and prestige of Athens were at their height.

On the subject of the election of the *strategoi* the "Old Oligarch" had this to say:

[T]here are many of these offices which, according as they are in good or in bad hands, are a source of safety or of danger to the People, and in these the People prudently abstains from sharing; as, for instance, it does not think it incumbent on itself to share in the functions of the general or of the commander of the cavalry . . . [but] recognizes the fact that in foregoing the personal exercise of these offices, and leaving them to the control of the more powerful citizens, it secures the balance of advantage to itself.

Robinson, 22-23

In the view of Thucydides, the most important contemporary writer, the system worked well so long as one man with the character and ability of Pericles was in control. Later leaders, who were personally ambitious and short-sighted, vied with one another in trying to sway the assembly. Without strong leadership consistent policy was impossible. Thucydides made this estimate of Pericles and the democracy:

Pericles, because of his position, his intelligence, and his known integrity, could respect the liberty of the people and at the same time hold them in check. It was he who led them, rather than they who led him, and, since he never sought power from any wrong motive, he was under no necessity of flattering them: in fact he was so highly respected that he was able to speak angrily to them and to contradict them. . . . So, in what was nominally a democracy, power was really in the hands of the first citizen. But his successors, who were more on a level with each other and each of whom aimed at occupying the first place, adopted methods of demogogy which resulted in their losing control over the actual conduct of affairs.

Thucydides, 163-164

Perhaps the aspect of Athenian government which seems most strange to twentieth century Americans is the law courts and trials. The basic principle of the administration of justice was that cases should be heard and decided by the sovereign citizen body. Jurors who heard the cases were drawn from an enormous panel of 6,000 citizens (a quorum of the assembly), a cross section of the entire citizenry. Juries, varying in number but all of them very large, were drawn from this panel. Trials lasted only one day. The large number of jurors and the duration of only one day were safeguards against bribery. Verdicts were decided by a simple majority. There was no government prosecutor. Any citizen in good standing could bring charges and prosecute. (The trial of Socrates is a good example.) There was a presiding magistrate, but he was not a judge. The large jury hearing the case was judge as well as jury. Motives for prosecution were sometimes undoubtedly political or for the purpose of personal revenge. Appeal to emotion and political considerations and the ability of the prosecutor of defendant to sway the jury by oratory were likely to be factors in deciding the outcome.

In such trials clearly there was a minimum of reference to law and precedent. Neither jury nor prosecutor was trained in the law. The jury first pronounced a verdict of guilty or not guilty, and then after further testimony from both sides announced a penalty. There was no appeal to a higher court. The verdict of the jury was the voice of the sovereign citizenry.

Although our word "democracy" is derived from the Greek, Athenian democracy was very different from the American system. Ancient Greeks believed that democracy was possible only in the *polis*, a small homogeneous unit. Their kind of democracy could not have existed in a large geographical area like the United States. From our point of view there were serious flaws in Athenian democracy. The absence of a supreme written constitution, judicial review, and a system of checks and balances contributed to a lack of consistency and seeming instability. The limited, exclusive nature of Athenian democracy was also contrary to twentieth century democratic ideals. It was pure democracy for a privileged minority only, the male citizens. Women, foreigners, and slaves were not included.

The most serious weakness in the ancient Greek *polis*, not only of Athens but of all the city-states, was the parochialism and particularism which prevented the creation of a united Hellenic state, a weakness that led to outside conquest, first by Macedonia, then by Rome.

Nevertheless, in spite of weaknesses and flaws, Athenian democracy showed remarkable vitality, self-confidence, and resourcefulness. The Athenian citizens were not disciplined and trained for war as were their Spartan foes in the Peloponnesian War, but they displayed remarkable resiliency and endurance in the face of reverses. After the war there was a reaction against the democracy but it was short lived and complete democracy was soon restored.

The years of the fifth and fourth centuries when Athenian democracy was at its height were a period of unparalleled creativity in art and literature. This was in large part a manifestation of devotion to the *polis* and to the democracy.

It was a period of brief duration. In the fourth century, after the disaster of the Peloponnesian War, came growing disillusionment and skepticism. The writers of that period, notably Plato, and to a lesser extent, Aristotle, were hostile to Periclean democracy.

THE *POLIS:* RELIGION, ART, DRAMA

In fifth century Athens the *polis* and religion were insepara-bly linked. The American concept of separation of church and state would have been incomprehensible to an Athenian. So close was the union of state and religion that, as W.K.C. Guthrie puts it, "Religion and patriotism were the same thing." Guthrie continues:

> To appreciate the situation, we must realize how completely identified were the state and its religion. It was not a case of making the Church subordinate to the State. There was no word for church at all, nor did such a thing exist apart from the state itself. The gods were worshipped at festivals which were state occasions, and participation in them was part of the ordi-nary duties and activities of a citizen as such.
>
> Guthrie, 82

The identification of religion with the *polis* meant also a close relationship between *polis* and art and drama, which were media for celebrating the gods. The state was the principal patron of architecture and art. Temples and theaters, which were associ-ated with religious cults, were built at public expense:

> The same men who levied taxes and approved treaties also su-pervised, maintained, and paid for public works. Art was meshed in with daily living, not set apart for occasional lei-sure-time or for the special enjoyment of rich collectors and aesthetes. Art was found in the temples, theaters, stoas, and cemeteries, not in museums.
>
> Finley, 152

Temples were the pre-eminent architectural achievement of the Greeks. Although the temples and the sculptures which adorned them were made to honor a particular deity, there was a universality about Greek architecture and sculpture since the institution of the *polis* was common to all of Hellas, as were many of the deities. The simple, perfectly proportioned Doric style of architecture was most common on mainland Greece and in the cities in the west. The Ionic style, with more slender columns and slightly more ornate capitals, was prevalent in the east. It was also found to a lesser extent on the mainland. As we have seen, temples were not built as places for religious congregations to gather for worship. Except for a statue of the deity and an altar, interiors were not important. Temples were designed to be viewed from out of doors.

Sculpture, which reached its height in the fifth and fourth centuries, was more innovative, graceful, and imaginative than in the archaic period. The sculptors of the classical period mastered the representation of the human figure. The most important examples of sculpture were statues of deities. In addition friezes ornamenting the pediments of the temples depicted in detail scenes from mythology and history. Since athletic contests were religious in nature Greek sculptors often portrayed the figures of athletes. There were some examples of portrait sculpture, but the Greeks were not as interested as the Romans in portraying particular human beings. Instead they made images of idealized human beings to portray the deities. Greek statues were greatly admired by the Roman conquerors who carried off many of the finest examples with the result that relatively few originals from the fifth and fourth century survive. Many of the statues we know only from Roman copies.

Of course there were examples of private art as well as public. Vases and other ceramic vessels, beautifully shaped and ornamented with pictures from mythology and everyday life, adorned private homes and served a variety of functional purposes.

The dazzling achievements in architecture and sculpture of Periclean Athens were the ultimate expression of civic pride. In the Periclean ideal, the glory of Athens was cultural as well as political. With buildings and sculptures Athenians symbolized the greatness of their city and glorified her victory over the Persians. Because older temples and other public buildings had been destroyed or severely damaged by the Persian invaders, much new building was needed. Such old buildings as had survived were torn down and replaced, with the result that little evidence of Athenian buildings before the Persian invasion remains.

This tremendous building program was financed partly from Athens' own resources, partly from the treasury of the Delian League and the Athenian Empire. It employed many skilled artisans and thereby increased prosperity. Members of the empire may have resented the expenditure of funds, but to later ages the remains of Periclean Athens, and in particular the Parthenon standing in its majesty atop the Acropolis, represent and preserve the glory of ancient Greece.

As with architecture and sculpture, Greek drama was a special manifestation of the artistic creativity of fifth century Athens. All of the tragedies we possess were written in that century by three poets—Aeschylus, Sophocles, and Euripides—whose lives spanned the century.

The origins of tragedy are obscure and a matter of some debate among scholars. Tragedy appears to have developed out of ritual dances and singing by a chorus in celebration of Dionysus, the god of wine. These celebrations were common to most of Greece, but it was in Athens that theater was invented as a highly original art form developed out of traditional material. Theater began when an actor introduced dialogue between himself and the chorus. Genuine drama became possible when Aeschylus introduced a second actor. Sophocles introduced a third. Thereafter innovation in the form of tragedy ceased. There were never more than three actors with speaking parts on the stage at one time. The chorus always remained in Greek tragedy, but in later years its importance diminished.

All performances were out of doors. Spectators sat on the side of a hill. By the fifth century large theaters of stone were built, with rows of stone seats along the hillside. In the center below was the orchestra (from the Greek word for dance). The orchestra was originally the threshing floor on which rural Greeks danced and sang in celebration of Dionysus. In the theaters of the fifth century the action of the play as well as the dancing and singing of the chorus took place on the circular orchestra floor. In the center was an altar to Dionysus. Behind the orchestra was the *skene,* a long building which furnished the background and from which the actors emerged. There was no scenery. The theaters were very large, the audiences enormous. The remarkable acoustical properties which made it possible for audiences of several thousands to hear every word are a source of wonder today.

The tragedies were produced in Athens at the annual dramatic festivals, of which the most important was the City Dionysia. The dramas to be shown were chosen by a board of judges in a competition in which any playwright might participate. The festivals, which attracted visitors from all over the Greek world, began with a colorful ceremonial procession in honor of Dionysus. The presentation of tragedies extended over three days. The festivals were civic affairs, planned and produced by Athenian citizens. The large choruses were made up of Athenian citizens, and over a period of years a sizable portion of the citizen body would have participated. Until the fourth century there were no professional actors. The costs of production were paid in part out of public funds, in part by wealthy citizens who paid a "liturgy."

The tragedies, which held the attention of huge audiences seated on stone benches for three successive days, were very different from modern dramatic productions. There was little action, and although murder and other acts of violence were often part of the plot, they occurred offstage. All parts were played by men and boys who wore masks.

The subject matter of tragedy was nearly always traditional, taken from legends and myths. Although drama began as religious ritual and the plots of the plays were often familiar to the audience, the manner in which the fifth century tragic poets used these materials was original and creative. They dealt with moral issues of universal and sometimes topical concern, often the same issues as those the philosophers of the fourth century confronted. The dramas reflected the intellectual ferment of the fifth century—questions about the contemporary significance of traditional religion and traditional values, conflict between the individual and familial values, conflict between the individual and the state, and questions of retribution and justice. The dramatic festivals continued throughout the years of the Peloponnesian War, and some dramas dealt with issues raised by the war. For example, the *Trojan Women* of Euripides dealt with the fate of the defenseless women after the capture of Troy by the victorious Greeks of Homeric legend. But an Athenian audience, viewing the ancient story while the news of the destruction of Melos was fresh, must have seen parallels between the treatment of the Trojans and the treatment of the people of Melos by Athens.

Altogether the three great tragic poets, Aeschylus, Sophocles, and Euripides, wrote about 300 plays, of which 33 survive. Those which survive show similarities but also distinctive traits of each writer. The productive years of Aeschylus, who fought at both Marathon and Salamis, were between 490 and 456 B.C., the period after the glorious victories over the Persians. His plays reflect some issues current in Periclean Athens, but from those which survive it appears that his larger interest was in attempting to resolve certain religious questions conflicts between divine justice and human law, and between the ways of the gods and the ways of humans. Aeschylus's characters are majestic, embodiments of abstractions rather than realistic portrayals of particular individuals.

Sophocles (496 to 406 B.C.) was a generation younger than Aeschylus. Like him he was active in the life of the *polis,* serving as a general in one military campaign. His dramas, which spanned the period from 468 to 406 B.C., dealt with conflicts similar to those of Aeschylus but his characters are far more human than those of his predecessor.

The third member of the trio, Euripides (c. 485 to 406 B.C.), was a younger contemporary of Sophocles. In his plays divine motivation is less important than human. He was interested in oppressed groups, including women and slaves, and showed deep psychological insights. He was not as popular with Athenian audiences as was Sophocles, but there was a tradition that Socrates attended the theater only when a play of Euripides was shown. Euripides was highly regarded by later generations, and to us he seems much more modern than Aeschylus and Sophocles.

Comedy was also a part of the dramatic competitions and festivals in Athens. What is called "Old Comedy" was uniquely the product of fifth century Athenian society and politics. Like tragedy, comedy had its origins in the worship of Dionysus and the celebration and processions connected with the harvest of grapes and the drinking of new wine. Remnants of the processions and ritual orgies and fertility rites associated with Dionysus were apparent in the comedies produced in Athens. There was little plot but what there was was hilarious lampoon of human folly and desire that only a fifth century Athenian could fully appreciate.

The only comic poet of the period whose plays have come down to us is Aristophanes (c. 446-388 B.C.), eleven of whose works survive. Most of his comedies were written and produced during the years of the Peloponnesian War. They were essentially political. No person living or dead was immune; political leaders were held up to ridicule, sometimes bitter. The fact that such plays were produced during war time is testimony to the freedom of speech which Athenians enjoyed. *The Knights* was a lampoon on Cleon, leader of the democratic faction; *The Wasps* a satire on the law courts. The last of the plays written during the war years, *Lysistrata,* is the one best known to modern readers. It was written after the Sicilian disaster and reflects Aristophanes' desire for peace. In it the women of Athens force negotiation by a general strike against their husbands, denying them sexual favors. The play ends with a great reconciliation between Athens and Sparta.

PROSE WRITING—HISTORY

Prose writing developed later than did poetry. Probably the finest examples of prose were the works of two historians of the fifth century, Herodotus and Thucydides, and the Dialogues of Plato in the following century.

Early Greeks had been satisfied with the Homeric poems and other legends of a heroic era as accounts of their past. Sixth century prose writing is now largely lost to us. One fragment which survives shows growing skepticism about the old legends. Hecataeus of Miletus is reported to have said: "What I write here is the account of what I believe to be true. For the stories the Greeks tell are many, and in my opinion ridiculous."

Herodotus (c. 480-430 B.C.), who quoted Hecataeus, was the author of the first great work of prose literature. It is a history of the Persian Wars, but more than that. Herodotus lived in Periclean Athens when he conceived the idea for his work. The theme is the struggle between east and west, which culminated in the war between the Persian Empire and the Hellenes. To gather first-hand information Herodotus traveled to Egypt and other parts of the Persian Empire. His work is a compendium of information about the diverse peoples and cultures of the empire and a narrative of events leading up to the war and finally of the major campaigns of the war. Interspersed are amusing and revealing anecdotes and digressions about local customs. A true Greek, Herodotus had a constantly inquiring mind. In fact the Greek word "historia" meant simply "inquiry."

Herodotus was indeed the "father of history." There was no established methodology for him to follow nor any previous works to use as models. In some respects he was naive, but he had the essentials of historical scholarship: an inquiring, critical mind and a desire to get at the truth insofar as it was possible.

He thought there were meanings and lessons to be learned from the past, and he wrote to instruct as well as to entertain.

His great successor, Thucydides (c. 460 to 400 B.C.), was more explicit about his belief that people could learn lessons from the past. In fact, he tells us that this is his reason for writing history. Herodotus reflects the optimism and self-confidence of Periclean Athens, Thucydides the increasing rationalism and skepticism of the latter part of the century under the destructive forces unleashed by the Peloponnesian War. Herodotus was more akin to Sophocles, Thucydides to Euripides.

Thucydides was an Athenian of good family. He was chosen as a *strategos* during the early stages of the war with Sparta and then exiled after the failure of a naval campaign which he commanded at Amphipolis. He began writing his history of the war soon after the outbreak of hostilities, recognizing, he said, its importance. After his exile he traveled and was probably an eyewitness of some of the events he described. He did not write his history to entertain or merely as a narrative of the war. He said his account was devoid of "romance." But he left an unforgettable and unmatched exploration of the causes of war and an analysis of human motivation and behavior and of the disintegrating and destructive effects of war on society.

Thucydides did not finish his history. He died a few years after the final defeat of Athens. Our information about the last years of the war comes principally from the *Hellenica* of Xenophon, a fourth century writer, inferior to Thucydides both as a historian and as a writer.

PHILOSOPHY AND SCIENCE

As we have seen, Greek philosophers of the archaic period were engaged primarily in speculation about the nature of the physical universe. During the fifth century the focus of philosophical thought changed to humanistic concerns, the nature of human life and ethical questions. Athens was the center of philosophy as she was of all cultural and intellectual life. The new direction was in part the result of the emptiness of traditional religion and the growing skepticism about the old gods. People turned to philosophy to fill the vacuum from the lack of satisfying religion. The increased participation of all citizens in government under the democracy also heightened interest in the principles of government. Because Socrates was the dominant figure in ushering in the new era it is customary to divide Greek philosophy into two periods, pre-Socratic and Socratic.

Before considering Socrates, however, some attention must be given to those contemporaries known as Sophists. (The word "sophist" meant literally "practitioner of knowledge.") The Sophists were not in reality a school of philosophers; they possessed no common set of principles. They were teachers who made a living by collecting fees from their lectures. The Sophists were skeptics who rejected the traditional gods and who taught that there were no absolute truths or ethical values. Ethical relativists, they held that all human activity was dictated by experience, that there were two sides to every question, and that any proposition could be argued both ways. It was commonly said that Sophists taught how "to make the worse appear the better." In an age when success in politics and the law courts depended in large part on rhetorical ability and oratory the Sophists attracted a following.

Quite unlike the Sophists, Socrates believed that there were absolute truths and that his mission was to discover them. One of his objectives was to refute the Sophists. Socrates was a teacher; he apparently wrote nothing. What we know of his life and philosophy comes principally from the remarkably life-like portrayal in the early Dialogues of Plato, but there are references to him in other writings, including Xenophon's *Memorabilia*. The Socrates of Plato's Dialogues claims he has no moral knowledge; he is wise simply in knowing that he does not know. But he has a divine mission to discover the truth. He seeks to obtain knowledge by endless questioning. His quest is for *arete,* a word usually translated as "virtue." A better translation probably is "excellence," and it could mean excellence in a variety of functions. For Socrates and his followers it was "human" *arete,* what constituted excellence in a person—that is, the human being's aim or function. His interest was in the moral nature of the person, but of the person as part of the *polis,* and how to achieve *arete* in the government of the *polis.*

Socrates argued that one could not talk about wisdom, justice, goodness, or other ethical terms without being able to define them. The first step toward the discovery of *arete* was to expose the ignorance of those who used these terms without being able to define them. Hence his inexorable questioning. He believed that people do not do wrong willfully, but only through ignorance. If they could be brought to see the truth they would automatically choose it.

Socrates' method was to have the person whom he was questioning (teaching) propose a definition or thesis, which Socrates would then pick apart. When the person being interrogated tried again, his argument was then demolished by Socrates until he was finally convinced of his ignorance. In the words of W.K.C. Guthrie, "The essence of the Socratic method is to convince the interlocutor that whereas he thought he knew something, in fact he does not. The conviction of ignorance is a necessary first step to the acquisition of knowledge" (Guthrie, 74).

It is not surprising that many Athenians did not feel comfortable with such a man and that they thought him arrogant although he was apparently genuinely humble. Nor is it surprising that people confused him and his teachings with the Sophists. His methods clearly had the effect of destroying some cherished, long-held beliefs and traditional views.

The reasons for the trial of Socrates are complex, but it occurred in the aftermath of Athens' defeat by Sparta. Athenians had lost their self-confidence and security. In such an atmosphere new ideas were viewed with suspicion and fear of their possible consequences. For example, to appear to question established religion was to appear to question the whole established order of society. Socrates was charged with not believing in the gods of the *polis* and with corrupting the youth of Athens. He was found guilty. It is probable that most of the jurors who voted to condemn him did not want to see him suffer the death sentence. But he refused to propose a lesser penalty when given the opportunity, so he was sentenced to die. He considered it a matter of conscience not to make a conciliatory defense and not to escape after the sentence was pronounced. He chose to die by drinking hemlock, and by his death he achieved a kind of immortality.

The sentencing of Socrates by one of the large popular law courts brought further disillusionment to Athenian intellectuals who were already pessimistic about the democracy and the state of the *polis*. Most notably the death of Socrates, whom he considered his master, had a profound effect on Plato.

Plato (427-347 B.C.) was an aristocrat who might have been expected to enter public life. He was, however, already disenchanted and somewhat disdainful of the democracy, and the death of Socrates was an important reason for his turning to a life of teaching, philosophy, and writing. One of the main purposes in his early Dialogues was to make people understand Socrates, his position and his motives. Plato opened a school, the Academy, about 387 B.C., where he lectured on mathematics, astronomy, and ethics. He is known best today for his Dialogues, writings in which he uses the dialectical method of logical argument to develop an idea. The central figure is always Socrates, but there is always the question of how much the argument is the true Socrates and how much it is Plato. The early Dialogues undoubtedly represent Socrates as Plato remembered him, while in the later Dialogues Socrates is more the invention of Plato. Plato was a brilliant writer, and the Dialogues make fascinating reading quite aside from the philosophical content.

Plato intended not merely to commemorate Socrates but also to attempt answers to some of the questions he had raised. Like Socrates he tried to establish the existence of absolutes to overcome the moral confusion of his times. His most famous Dialogue, *The Republic,* is such an effort. Plato tries to create an ideal, rational and "just" state. The discussion is not merely about the fairness of the legal system but also about the right ordering of things in the *polis,* the achievement of *arete* in government. Plato rejects the ideal of Periclean democracy because in it power lay with persons who lacked the education necessary for excellence in government.

Plato accepted the basic inequality of human beings. He thought that government should be placed in the hands of the few men who were morally superior, his "philosopher kings."

He believed that absolute truths and absolute good could be known only to a few through the right system of education. One of the most interesting aspects of *The Republic* is the emphasis Plato places on education. In this state the individual would be subordinated to the common good, and justice and harmony would be achieved by the individual citizen's assignment to a function according to character and ability.

Plato lived for eighty-one years and was a voluminous writer. His works are too immense, complex, and sometimes abstract for any kind of brief summary, but he raised questions and formulated concepts and methods which have been central to much of western philosophy to the present time.

The most famous pupil at Plato's Academy was Aristotle (384-322 B.C.) who, after Plato's death, founded his own school in Athens, the Lyceum. Aristotle's thought took a different direction from that of Plato. Aristotle was by nature an organizer and classifier. More than any other person he originated the content and organization of western thought and scholarship. The fact that his father was court physician to the king of Macedon may have caused his interest to turn to science, and to biology in particular. Early in his career he spent time examining and classifying biological phenomena, and he applied similar methods to other fields of knowledge, including politics and literature.

Aristotle did not believe, like Plato, that there was one universal truth but he did believe that nothing exists without a reason, that everything has an end or purpose (*telos*) for which it was created. His interests were encyclopedic and he wrote on a great variety of subjects. He did not use the dialectical form of Plato and he did not compare with his predecessor in literary ability. His works are treatises or essays, only a fraction of which survive, some of them probably lecture notes which he prepared for use in the Lyceum. Some of his works were apparently compendiums of research done by his students.

He believed that knowledge as a whole was made up of various categories and that there was a particular methodology for each. His great contribution was an attempt to systemize all this. He viewed logic as a instrument, a preliminary to the study of every branch of knowledge. His tracts on logic dealt with various kinds of reasoning: "Philosophy, as it appeared to him, was an attempt to explain the natural world, and if it could not do so, ... then it must be considered to have failed" (Guthrie, 125). He believed that knowledge should be useful as well as theoretical. In his *Ethics,* for example, he says: "The present inquiry does not aim at knowledge like our others. Its object is not that we may know what virtue is, but that we may become virtuous" (Guthrie, 151).

In the treatise on *Politics* Aristotle, like Plato, dealt with the *polis* as the ideal form of government even though by the time he wrote, its independence was being destroyed. The *Politics* opens with the statement:

> Every *polis* is a community of some kind, and every community is established for the sake of some good. (For everyone does everything for the sake of what seems good.) But while all communities aim at some good, the supreme and overarching

> community, which includes all others, will aim at the highest
> good. This is what we call the *polis.*
>
> Aristotle, Politics, I, 1

Aristotle viewed the individual as a political animal. Human
behavior was connected with the nature of the state and politics.

The *Politics,* a very different work from Plato's *Republic,* was
drawn from an analysis of existing political institutions which he
and his pupils had prepared on the constitutional history and
working of government of 158 states. In the *Poetics* Aristotle
turned to the critical investigation of literature. He used the
methods of empirical descriptive analysis similar to those he had
applied to natural phenomena. His analysis of epic poetry and
tragedy has influenced the standards by which these forms of
literature are judged even today. The *Rhetoric,* which analyzed
and organized public speaking into categories, also has had a
lasting influence.

As we have seen, the ancient Greeks made no distinction
between philosophy and science. Both Plato and Aristotle made
important contributions in fields of scholarship which today
would be regarded as more "scientific" than "philosophical."
Pupils in the Academy and the Lyceum investigated scientific
subjects. Plato was deeply interested in mathematics. All of the
most important mathematical work of the fourth century was
done by Plato and his pupils, and Plato's great contribution to
science was the application of mathematics to science, especially
to astronomy.

Aristotle was interested in biology, and the atmosphere and
methods in the Lyceum were in some ways more "scientific"
than "philosophical." He created much scientific terminology.
His treatises rested on collection, observation, and classification
of natural phenomena. He failed, however, to carry out certain
tests that would have shown the inaccuracy of some of his
propositions. Biological treatises make up more than one fifth of
Aristotle's writings. The aim of natural science in his view was to
find the causes of phenomena. In his *Study of Animals* he ex-
plained both his objectives and his methods. Observation of the

external parts of animals was not sufficient; it should be supplemented by vivisection.

Other scholars of the fifth and fourth centuries made significant progress in the development of medical science. There were no legally recognized qualifications for the practice of medicine but there were men with specialized knowledge. While the mass of people probably continued to believe that disease could be expelled by charms or visits to sacred shrines, these men rejected superstition and the supernatural as causes and cures. The most celebrated physician was Hippocrates (c. 460-377 B.C.) from the island of Cos. Hippocrates believed that every illness has a natural cause. A body of treatises preserved from the fifth century, known as the Hippocratic Corpus, throws light on medical knowledge and practice. The Corpus includes treatises on observation, diagnosis, and treatment of disease. Treatments described include hygiene, diet, exercise, surgery, blood-letting, and administering of purgative drugs.

The greatest achievements in ancient Greek science were in astronomy. Much of the early knowledge may have been transmitted directly or indirectly from discoveries made in Babylonia. With Greeks, as with other early peoples, the need to regulate the calendar and the needs of farmers created practical as well as theoretical reasons for the study of the heavenly bodies. Plato insisted that astronomy was an exact mathematical science. Later research rested on his theories.

The most impressive and lasting achievements of Greek mathematics, astronomy, and physical science and physical geography belong to the Hellenistic era, the period following the conquests of Alexander the Great. Greek scholars carried on their research in new centers of learning such as Alexandria in Egypt.

Among the great names was Euclid of Alexandria (c. 300 B.C.) whose chief work, *Elements,* was a textbook on geometry so precise and logical that little improvement has ever been made upon it. The main interest of Archimedes of Syracuse (c. 287 to 212 B.C.) was pure mathematics, but he is best remembered for his achievements in applied science. He was the founder of mechanics and hydrostatics. Eratosthenes (c. 275 to 195 B.C.) was able to compute the circumference of the earth quite accurately and to theorize that it might be possible to reach India by sailing westward across the Atlantic Ocean. Aristarchos of Samos (c. 310 to 230 B.C.) brought astronomy to the highest point achieved by the ancients when he propounded the heliocentric theory of the universe, the theory that the earth revolved around the sun. Little was added to the discoveries of these ancients until the early modern era, and modern science rests on their contributions.

In assessing the contributions of the ancient Greeks of the classical period to science it is necessary to recognize differences between the ancient and modern world. In the first place, Greek science was "aristocratic" in the sense that it was the domain of the few. Scientific research did not bring financial rewards, although a few men made a livelihood through medicine and lecturing on scientific subjects. But most people who were engaged in philosophy and science were independently wealthy or were subsidized by wealthy patrons. This meant that there was little interest in or incentive for applying science to practical uses. The widely held conviction of the modern world that science and technology hold the key to human progress was quite alien to the ancient Greeks.

The fundamental contribution of the Greeks to science might be called the beginning of the "scientific point of view," an attempt to look for rational rather than supernatural causes and explanations. They recognized what the problems were, although they were sometimes unable to supply answers. They developed two methodological principles on which modern science rests: the application of mathematics to understanding natural phenomena and the method of empirical research—careful observation and recording of data. It is not true, as some writers have claimed, that the Greeks did not engage in scientific experimentation, but the use of such methods was limited until the Hellenistic era. As G.E.R. Lloyd, a distinguished modern scholar, says: "The impression that much of the history of early Greek science leaves is one of the dominant role of abstract argument" (Lloyd, 142).

AFTERMATH

The Hellenistic Era

At the end of the Peloponnesian War Sparta was victorious and Athens, defeated and exhausted, was deprived of her empire and most of her fleet. But the period of Spartan domination was short-lived. After her defeat Athens showed a remarkable recovery. She formed a new voluntary confederacy with some members of her former empire. Athens remained the cultural center of the Greek world. The democracy was restored, but there was a decline in the vitality of the *polis* and a decline in self-confidence.

No single city was sufficiently powerful to lead and unite the Greeks. Instead much of the fourth century was a dreary succession of inter-city wars, an unstable situation which invited intervention and domination from the outside.

Macedonia, a kingdom on the northern border of Greece, was developing into a strong military power. The Macedonians were akin to the Greeks and spoke the same language, but were culturally less developed. Rulers of Macedonia admired Greek culture and invited scholars and writers to their court. For example, Aristotle spent some years as tutor to Alexander, the heir to the throne.

Alexander's father, Philip, who ruled from 359 to 336 B.C., was a remarkably able man who, by diplomacy, bribery, and finally by armed conquest, gained control over most of Greece. In Athens one faction urged cooperation with Philip. Another, led by the famous orator Demosthenes, urged armed resistance. At the battle of Chaeronea (338 B.C.) Philip was victorious over Athens. After this Macedonia was dominant in mainland Greece.

For the most part Philip and his successors allowed the Greek city-states to retain their old institutions, but the era when the *polis* was the center of Greek life and culture had ended.

Philip's achievements were overshadowed by the spectacular conquests of his son Alexander, who in a few short years changed the course of history as few individuals have ever done. In thirteen years (336 to 323 B.C.) Alexander conquered the far-flung Persian Empire, including Egypt, a domain that stretched from the Aegean to India. For a long time the Persian Empire had been decaying from within. Although Alexander was a military genius aided by some very fine generals, his victories were due in part to the weakness of his opponents. During the course of his campaigns Alexander destroyed some older cities and founded eighteen or twenty new ones—all called Alexandria. Thousands of Macedonians and Greeks—soldiers and civilians—flocked to these new settlements and to garrisons which Alexander built.

Within a few years Alexander's empire was fragmented. After his death his generals began to fight among themselves and to divide his conquests. In Egypt Ptolemy established a dynasty which ruled until the conquest by Rome. Seleucus gained control of much of the Asian portion of the Persian Empire. Macedonia was ruled by the Antigonid dynasty, which was descended from another of Alexander's generals. These three states, which fought constantly among themselves, were the principal powers of the Hellenistic world.

The term Hellenistic is used to designate the period from Alexander to the conquest of the eastern Mediterranean world by Rome, a period very different from the classical period although the influence of classical Greece remained strong.

In the Hellenistic period the centers of power and culture shifted away from mainland Greece. The three great powers were large territorial states ruled by absolute monarchs. Like Alexander these rulers founded new cities in Asia and Egypt to which large numbers of Greeks migrated as mercenary soldiers, merchants, artisans, businessmen, and government administrators. Some of the new cities, notably Alexandria in Egypt and

Pergamum in Asia Minor, became the principal centers of scholarship and art. In their new environment Greeks, who were a privileged class, preserved and disseminated classical Greek culture and institutions. They built temples and theaters and carried on religious festivals and athletic contests. Classical Greek remained the language of literature, and a new simplified form of Greek (*koine*) became a kind of universal written and spoken language throughout the Hellenistic world. Although they retained much of their Hellenism, Greeks who settled in new lands also mingled with the local people, sometimes intermarrying, and absorbed some of their institutions and ideas. Hellenistic culture was in reality a fusion of classical Greek and eastern cultures. The Hellenistic world was a cosmopolitan society in which people, commerce, and ideas moved freely. The extreme particularism which had characterized the independent city-states of classical Greece declined.

These changes were especially apparent in philosophy and religion. As we have seen, the concept of the independent *polis* was important in the thought of Plato and Aristotle. In the Hellenistic era new schools of philosophy with different perspectives emerged. The most influential was Stoicism, which transcended the city-state and taught the brotherhood of all men. Greeks continued to worship the Olympian gods and to hold traditional religious ceremonies. But they were also influenced by the religious cults of the east and absorbed many elements from them, particularly those of the mystery religions. The outlook of Hellenistic religion became increasingly mystical and other-worldly.

By 30 B.C. all of the eastern Mediterranean world had been conquered by Rome. First, through contacts with the Greek colonies in the west, later through conquest and knowledge of old Greece, Romans absorbed and imitated much of Greek culture in their religion, literature, architecture, and art. In turn they preserved, modified, and transmitted this legacy to later ages.

WORKS CITED

Aristotle, *The Politics,* selections translated from the Greek for this edition by Paula Reiner, Department of Classics, Butler University.

Ehrenberg, Victor, *The Greek State,* Oxford: B. Blackwell, 1960.

Finley, M.I., *The Ancient Greeks,* New York: Penguin Books, 1963.

Guthrie, W. K. C. (William Keith Chambers), *The Greek Philosophers from Thales to Aristotle,* New York: Harper & Row, 1975.

Homer, *Iliad,* Robert Fitzgerald, translator, Garden City, New York: Doubleday & Company, 1961.

Homer, *Odyssey,* Book I, Richmond Lattimore, translator, New York: Harper & Row, 1967.

Kitto, H. D. F. (Humphrey Davy Findley), *The Greeks,* New York: Penguin, 1986.

Lloyd, G. E. R. (Geoffrey Ernest Richard), *Early Greek Science: Thales to Aristotle,* New York, W.W. Norton & Company: 1970.

Pollitt, J. J. (Jerome Jordan), *Art and Experience in Classical Greece,* New York: Cambridge University Press, 1972.

Robinson, Charles Alexander, Jr., *Athens in the Age of Pericles,* Norman, Oklahoma: University of Oklahoma Press, 1959.

Thucydides, *The Peloponnesian War,* trans. Rex Warner, London: Penguin, 1954.